Scriptures for the Church Seasons

Lent 2009
Come to the Cross

John Indermark

A Lenten Study Based on the Revised Common Lectionary

Abingdon Press

A Lenten Study Based on the Revised Common Lectionary

COME TO THE CROSS

Copyright © 2008 by Abingdon Press

Scripture quotations in this publication, unless otherwise indicated, are from the New Revised Standard Version of the Bible, copyright 1989, Division of Christian Education of the National Council of the Churches of Christ in the United States of America. Used by permission. All rights reserved.

All readings taken from the Revised Common Lectionary © 1992 Consultation on Common Texts are used by permission.

ISBN-13: 978-0-687-64808-5

Manufactured in the United States of America

08   09   10   11   12   13   14   15   16   17—10   9   8   7   6   5   4   3   2   1

Contents

Introduction

Lent provides a season in which the church journeys with Jesus toward Jerusalem. Like Advent, Lent offers a time of preparation. Unlike Advent, Lent's climax does not come in a birthing but in a dying and a rising. There is always the temptation to bypass the somber notes of this season and rush straight from Ash Wednesday to Easter morning. "Alleluias" sing easier than "Were you there when they crucified my Lord?" Yet the impact of an empty tomb is most fully experienced when we witness again the Passion of Jesus and when we keep vigil at the cross.

COME TO THE CROSS offers you the opportunity and challenge to journey toward Jerusalem and the cross. It does so through exploring the lectionary readings designated for this Lenten season. The Gospel texts provide insight into the original journey made by Jesus and his followers. Those insights come sometimes in narrations of life along the way, sometimes in teachings about the cross. The Epistle readings offer reflections on that journey from the early Christian community. The Old Testament passages provide landmarks experienced by the people of God that helped them and help us understand Jesus' journey to the cross.

Pay attention to the wording of the title of this study: COME TO THE CROSS. *Come* is an imperative verb that issues an invitation, a summons. The cross is not a peripheral afterthought of Christian theology. The cross stands at the core of how we understand the character of God's love and discipleship. We might prefer that our faith would take us to places other than the cross in order to learn about God or about following Jesus. If you wonder about that, consider contemporary appeals to faith that would center relationship with God in the fruits of material prosperity or national well-being. In the Epistle reading for the third Sunday in Lent, Paul uses a revealing phrase to speak of Christ crucified: *stumbling block* (1 Corinthians 1:23). The Greek word there is *skandalon*, from which we get *scandal.*

COME TO THE CROSS invites us to the scandal of following a Messiah who came not to inflict suffering on enemies unto death but to love enemies for the sake of their (our) life. Come to the Cross invites us to the scandal of trusting God for life even when appearances point to God-forsaken death. Come to the cross.

Water Words

Scriptures for Lent:
The First Sunday
Genesis 9:8-17
1 Peter 3:18-22
Mark 1:9-15

Waters are a powerful symbol in Judaism and Christianity. Two distinct traditions about waters influence the biblical perspective. The first traditions parallel belief in the civilizations that arose in the flood plains of Egypt and Mesopotamia, where waters were a threat to life that must be controlled. In stories that echo Genesis 1, the waters there were an enemy that God had to conquer. God's punishment of a creation gone sour in the time of Noah occurred by allowing the waters to do their natural thing by rising up and swallowing life. Those ideas find their way into segments of the New Testament. When disciples saw Jesus walking across the waters of Galilee, Matthew and Mark recorded their initial reaction of believing it was a ghost. When Revelation 21 provides its vision of a new heaven and a new earth, it declares, "And the sea was no more." God did away with the waters.

A second and different tradition of waters exists in the biblical material. The communities scattered in the more arid regions of Palestine viewed water as a gift and a source of life. In Genesis 1, creation emerges by God's Spirit moving upon the waters. In Exodus, the waters become the means of Israel's escape from slavery in Egypt. In the wilderness, in spite of the people's murmuring and bickering, God graced Israel with life by the gift of water when Moses struck the rock with his staff. In exile, the people of Israel were promised streams flowing through the desert to sustain them on their journey home.

Nowhere is that positive imagery of the waters so pronounced as in baptism. The waters poured out upon us and over us are the waters that clean and renew, that bestow us with name, grace, and calling. In the story of Jesus' baptism, Jesus received the confirmation of his identity among us: the beloved Son, with whom God is well-pleased. Baptism ushers in his ministry. In these waters, we too are named or, to use an older expression, *christened*. In the waters of baptism, our life is united with the life of the One whom John baptized. The waters of baptism convey the grace of salvation and identity. We are who God says we are: an identity that leads to vocation and ministry. To live as God's child is to live respectfully and lovingly toward the other children in the family.

Water words run through each of today's Scriptures. Out of the disaster of flood, God offered the sign of the bow for covenant with all creation. The First Epistle of Peter links traditions of the Flood to proclaim Christ's grace for the living and the dead. Mark blended a watered benediction pronounced on Jesus at baptism with wilderness preparations for gospel ministry. Let us follow these water words with our first steps as we come to the cross.

A COVENANTING WORD
GENESIS 9:8-17

The waters had receded. The ark that carried Noah and the animals had safely come to rest, and they set foot on dry ground for the first time in a year. Noah built an altar and made sacrifices. Words arose in the heart of God incredible in their promise and in their perspective: "I will never again curse the ground because of humankind, for the inclination of the human heart is evil from youth" (Genesis 8:21b).

If you go back to Genesis 6:5-7, the inclination of the human heart toward evil was the reason given for the destruction unleashed in the Flood. What had grieved the heart of God (6:6) then gave rise to God's covenant promise of "never again."

In the ancient Near East, covenants were agreements entered into by two parties, often between rulers and subjects or between two nations of disproportionate power or standing. Covenants defined the relationship between the two partners. In unequal covenants, that relationship often came to be described in a historical "prologue" that established their standing toward one another and what obligated the "lesser" to serve the "greater." Those obligations could be stated in legal terms, along with addendums of blessings for following the prescribed course and curses for neglecting the covenant obligations. We may be most familiar with such terms and conditions in the covenant of Sinai or Moses.

The Mosaic covenant founded the relationship between Israel and God, and the covenant God entered with Noah struck a far broader base. Look at the covenant partners identified by Genesis 9. Verse 9 speaks of Noah and his sons and their descendants. Given the narrative of the extent of the Flood's prior destruction, this amounts to all human creation; but the partners of covenant do not stop there. Verse 10 speaks of God's covenanting with "every living creature that is with you." As if that is not stretching the limits of God's covenant partners, consider verse 13: "I have set my bow in the clouds, and it shall be a sign of the covenant between me and the earth."

Take a deep breath, and imagine the canvas upon which God paints the mural of covenant. It embraces all humanity. It includes every living creature. It encompasses the whole earth. God covenants with all. There are no afterthoughts at the end of the passage of *Oh wait, I really didn't mean to include THAT region or THESE creatures or THOSE people.* The covenant overarches all. One wonders if Paul might have had a "back to the future" theme in mind when he wrote much later of God's plan in Christ to "gather up all things in him, things in heaven and things on earth" (Ephesians 1:10). The gathering of all things by God at the end mirrors God's covenanting with all things at the beginning.

Earlier it was noted that many covenants stated obligations or conditions. That is, do these things; and all will be well. Slip up, and you will face the consequences. If the breadth of the Noah covenant amazes, its conditions surprise because there are none. There are no ifs in this covenant. There are no duties placed upon God's partners whose keeping will be required for the promises to be kept. This covenant is unconditional. "Never again" is not joined to any "unless." God enacts this covenant: extravagantly in scope, graciously in effect. It is God's gift to the world. The conclusive water words spoken in the wake of the Flood are not warning but grace.

The covenant with Noah contains what may be the most famous of all biblical signs: the rainbow. The sign is given when it rains, the time when risk may be felt or trust may be tested. The fascinating truth about the sign of the bow in Genesis 9 is this: It is to be a sign for the sake of God. "When I bring clouds over the earth and the bow is seen in the clouds, I will remember my covenant. . . . When the bow is in the clouds, I will see it and remember the everlasting covenant" (verses 14-15a, 16a). Twice the author of Genesis indicated the bow is a sign meant to evoke God's remembrance of covenant, of humanity and every living creature and the earth, of "never again." The sign spurs our trust by reminding us God may be trusted to remember, to keep covenant as graciously as God has enacted covenant.

What do these water words of expansive covenant and gracious sign have to do with "Come to the Cross"? The cross is all about the gracious initiative of God. The reality of the human heart is not the rationale for God's judgment but the motivation for God to act with radical graciousness. The *all* included in Noah's covenant corresponds to the *all* extended grace in the cross of Jesus. What about the cross as sign? To be sure, the cross reminds us of the extent to which God's love goes for the sake of our lives. Beyond that, however, might we also see, as in the Noah covenant, the cross as a sign that brings to God's remembrance the truth and depth of such love and mercy?

The relationship God established in the Genesis 9 covenant anticipates the relationship God seeks in the cross: a relationship radical in its inclusion, extravagant in its grace, and never-ending in its term.

May the rainbow and the cross bear witness to the depth and breadth of God's love for all creation!

Where does the covenant with Noah speak most deeply to you: in your relationship with God, in your valuing of the earth and its creatures? In what ways does the unconditional nature of the Noah covenant reflect your spiritual journey and experiences? What signs do you carry that remind you of God's grace and trustworthiness?

A SAVING WORD
1 PETER 3:18-22

Before attending to the water words in 1 Peter 3 concerning baptism, attention needs to be paid to an underlying theme of the entire epistle that comes to the fore in this text: suffering. Throughout First Peter we find the verb *pascho* (from which we get *passion*) that means "suffering" or "enduring." Suffering is not simply a thematic concern for the author of First Peter. Suffering represents the precarious condition of those to whom the epistle was originally addressed.

With suffering as the backdrop, First Peter identifies itself as a letter intended to encourage the followers of Jesus. This dual theme of suffering and encouragement recalls a passage from Isaiah 43:2a that, interestingly, poses God's support with words borne of water: "When you pass through the waters, I will be with you; / and through the rivers, they shall not overwhelm you."

So when our Scripture lifts up the suffering of Christ, it serves two purposes. First, it creates a bridge of community between Christ and the church addressed in these words. The One we follow is not removed from the harsh realities of our lives. Our suffering is not alien to God in Jesus but intrinsic to the ministry of Jesus among us.

Second, an important distinction is drawn in that identification. The suffering endured by the community addressed by this epistle, and many since, is ongoing. We hope we will find an end to it, but that hope may not be realized in our lifetime. In contrast, the epistle asserts that Christ's suffering is "once and for all." That is, the suffering endured in Jesus' Passion and cross does not go on and on and on indefinitely. The cross is decisive in its revealing of the love and forgiveness of God. The cross is necessarily paired with the Resurrection (1 Peter 3:22), for the Resurrection affirms that the reach and risk of God's love revealed in the cross triumphs over the powers of sin and death. We should read the word *powers* in the previous sentence not only as the forces at work within our lives but as those forces abroad in the world who choose to live by the threat and imposition of death.

The passage takes this affirmation further down the road of mystery when it speaks of Christ making "proclamation to the spirits in prison" (verse 19), following it with a reference to the days of Noah. Later in this epistle another reference will be made to the gospel being "proclaimed even to the dead" (4:6). What does that specifically mean? How is that related to the language in the

Apostles' Creed of Jesus "descending into hell"? Those who claim clear vivid answers speak outside of what the text reveals. What does seem clear is this: God's love and desire to save surpasses boundaries even we cannot imagine.

That desire and purpose to save becomes the focus of the final verses in this passage that speak of the water words of baptism. The author of First Peter makes this transition from those saved through water by Noah's ark to those saved by baptism. Is the epistle arguing that baptism as a rite saves? That does not seem to be the point here. It is simply the epistle drawing a comparison between the experience of the ark and that of baptism. In both, God's saving purposes are revealed in water; and in both, on a deeper level, God's saving purposes invite human response. God did not build the ark for Noah. Noah had to trust the message received and act upon it.

Likewise, baptism in First Peter is framed as an "appeal," that is, it invites us to make a response. In the language of the text, what is summoned is a "good conscience." That word in Greek literally means "a knowing of oneself." To know ourselves in baptism is to know ourselves called of God and made alive by God's Spirit. Baptism invites our consent and even beyond our consent, our decision to live this grace entrusted to us. Perhaps not coincidentally, the author of First Peter uses *conscience* in 3:16, where it is joined to our "good conduct in Christ." Baptism invites us to live the new life in Christ, trusting in the power of the resurrection of Jesus Christ to make this new life possible.

We come to the cross, not to resign ourselves to suffering and death but to trust in God's purposes for life. We come to the cross to experience more deeply how our baptism unites us in Christ's death and in Christ's life. We come to the cross as those who would trust and follow Jesus in how we live. We come to the cross, for here we see the saving purposes of God.

What has helped you understand the meaning of Christ's suffering as it relates to sin? as it relates to your own suffering and that of others? In what ways have you experienced the boundary-breaking powers of Christ's love in your life? in your faith community? What appeal does baptism make to you in the promises you may have made at baptism or confirmation? in the experience of witnessing baptism as part of a community?

A WILDERNESS WORD
MARK 1:9-15

The first of the Lenten Gospel texts, curiously, is not set on the final trip to Jerusalem when Jesus teaches about the necessity and meaning of his suffering. Rather, it comes at the beginning of Jesus' ministry following his baptism by John: "The Spirit immediately drove him out into the wilderness. He was in the wilderness forty days, tempted by Satan" (Mark 1:12-13). There are no infancy narratives in Mark's Gospel. The sequence of Mark's opening moves quickly in our text. John the Baptizer cried out in the wilderness, and Jesus came to the waters of the

Jordan. Notice this, though: The baptismal words pronounced upon Jesus as the Beloved with whom God is well-pleased resulted immediately in the Spirit's driving Jesus into the wilderness. Before Christ entered public ministry, he first had to confront a time alone in the desert.

Jesus' wilderness sojourn evokes Israel's own history. Between deliverance from Egypt and entrance into the Promised Land, Israel had known the desert as home for 40 years. Israel's wilderness sojourn was also a time of testing—a time of determining what lay within, a time of learning the source of what (and Who) sustains life. In the case of Jesus, the benediction of "beloved" and "well-pleased" as he emerged from the waters were tested in arid desert.

There is irony in a chapter on water words having wilderness play such a key role in its Gospel reading. The Judean wilderness was noted for its extreme scarcity of water—potable or otherwise. Mark offers an abbreviated account of Jesus' time in the desert. Matthew and Luke tell the story in greater detail, expanding on the specifics of the testings or temptations put to Jesus. What all share in common, however, is the setting: wilderness. Wilderness offers a place where the ordinary social and community sources of support are removed or suspended. Wilderness serves as the setting where traditions and values can be tested by eliminating the structures that normally mediate them to us. In the wilderness, solitude can easily change into loneliness. In the wilderness, living can be reduced to mere survival.

In our generation, wilderness has become something of a contested arena on the political front. Those who would preserve raw stretches of forests and rivers wrestle with those who would seek multiple-use of the resources contained there. However, the wilderness as it relates to our lives in the light of this text is not a political football. Instead, wilderness refers here to times and places where we find ourselves far removed from the ordinary supports of family and community and neighborhood convenience stores. Wilderness provides the settings, be they in national park vistas or urban environments, where we experience the solitude of standing alone and the possibility of recognizing holy ground. Wilderness strips away pretensions and assumptions and forces us to look deep inside at who we are—and whose we are—in order to understand our place in life.

Neither Mark nor the other Gospel writers link Jesus' time of wilderness with that of the cross, but they easily could have. The word of the cross is, at its heart, a word that belongs in spirit to the wilderness. It is a word whose experience is not unlike what Jesus knew in his sojourn of 40 days. The cross was indeed a time of testing: testing the limits of love, testing the limits of forgiveness. It is one thing to speak of love of neighbor and even enemy as a teacher when all that is at stake is words or an academic debate. It is quite another to offer love and forgiveness to those who not only misunderstand but crucify. The cross tests the very grace of God by revealing the depths to which it will go for our sake.

Like the wilderness, the cross was a place where ordinary human support was suspended, where community was reduced to speechless grief or the ridicule of insensitive tongues. Yet, from the cross, Jesus spoke words of forgiveness to tormentors. From the cross, Jesus entrusted the care of mother and friend to one another. As Jesus refused to allow the cross to destroy his community with others and their caring for one another, so does the cross become a sign of the power of human relationship enriched by the presence of grace. In the cross, Jesus does not allow life to be reduced to mere survival. As some of Jesus' detractors noted with cruel intentions: If he were God's Son or Israel's king, he would come down off the cross. If Jesus trusted in God, then God should rescue him. None of that happens because what is at stake is not survival but mission. Mission entails faithfulness to God's purposes for life even in the face and experience of death.

So it was for Jesus. So it is for us. Decision about faith arises in the wilderness. Wilderness as encountered in this text and in our lives is not the tamed and domesticated wilderness sought by weekend retreats to campgrounds more brightly lit by Coleman lanterns and Honda generators than many shopping-mall parking lots. The wilderness Jesus entered and faced involved separation from all that was familiar, from all the protections and comforts afforded by society. The wilderness times in our lives are not defined by National Forest Service boundaries. Wilderness times come when we have felt uprooted and separated from the persons and places we have ordinarily depended on for our moorings and bearings. Such times test our values and commitments, whether they are intrinsic to us or simply excess baggage that can be discarded when push comes to shove. To have known such times in our lives is to identify with what Jesus faced in the wilderness and later at the cross.

To have known such times in our lives is to be opened to the help and strength that can be found in the grace of God. For when Mark concluded Jesus' wilderness story, he added at the end that the angels "waited" on him. The Greek verb there is *diakoneo*, the most frequently used verb in the New Testament and the early church for "ministry." When we enter those times and places of wilderness in our lives, like Jesus, we experience God not in abandonment but in ministry. Like Israel of old, God feeds us in the wilderness.

That does not mean faith allows escape from wilderness or avoidance of its testings. Discipleship that follows the way of Jesus will inevitably encounter such times and places. Indeed, as this Scripture makes clear at the beginning, God's Spirit *drove* Jesus into the wilderness. There is a sense here of God compelling Jesus to experience wilderness so that when such times and challenges come in the way that leads to Jerusalem and the cross, trust may be kept and ministry may be exercised. It is possible that experiences of wilderness in our faith journeys may play a similar role: to prepare us, to teach us not self-sufficiency but God-sufficiency, and to reveal that solitude can bring deeper experiences of community and empowerment for new life.

Such empowerment moves seamlessly in this passage from Jesus' finding ministry from God's angels to Jesus' engaging in public ministry. Imagine how that speaks to the church as a whole and to you and me as followers of Jesus. The expression of God's love and favor lead directly and immediately to wilderness preparation and gospel proclamation. Those beloved of God are those sent by God: to discern in the wilderness what trust in God means, to exercise in our places of living what ministry such trust compels us toward.

The invitation to come to the cross is given first response by our willingness to join Jesus in those places where we learn radical reliance on grace and then to exercise that reliance in ministry and service that mediates that grace. Why? Because we, like Jesus, can then live with the conviction that the sovereign realm of God has come near. The water's benediction upon Jesus as God's beloved and favored rests upon us as well. Those words compel us to trust and service radically reliant on God and graciously extended to others. The good news is not just a gift; it is also a call.

Come to the waters, come to the wilderness, that you may learn what it means to come to the cross.

What have been the wilderness times in your life? How did you experience God within them or as a result of them? In what ways does your trust of God find expression in your service of others?

Following Calls

Scriptures for Lent:
The Second Sunday
Genesis 17:1-7, 15-16
Romans 4:13-25
Mark 8:31-38

Call is a word tossed around in religious circles with some frequency. We speak of our "call" as Christians. Congregations seek to understand our "call" to be in ministry and mission in particular places. Those in ordained ministry have traditionally been examined as to one's "call" to ministry. Calls are experienced in what we find ourselves urged or summoned, compelled or drawn to do in our lives.

Calls may take time to discern. I remember some events in the years leading up to my own decision to enter ordained parish ministry that, in hindsight, moved me in that direction. However, unlike some of my colleagues, the call did not come wrapped up neat and clean in one incident or a single heavenly voice that erased all doubts and made everything clear. The same remained true when the shape of my ministry shifted from full-time parish work toward a ministry of writing that now forms my vocation. Writing curricula and books is not the path of ministry and calling I set out consciously to follow when I knelt before the altar of Salvator Evangelical and Reformed United Church of Christ in 1976, but it has become so.

What is your understanding and experience of call and calling: when it comes to the practice of your life's work; when it comes to the perception of the gifts God has graced you with and the purposes that might best put them to good use? You may have noted that I used another word in the previous paragraph to speak of the work that issues from call: *vocation.* For some, vocation may sound quite ordinary in comparison to calling. Vocation may be taken as simply a synonym for *job*, but vocation has a deeper meaning. Look at the word itself. What do you see, especially in its prefix? *Vocation* comes from the same root as *vocal* or *voice*. To practice a vocation involves responding to and following what one has heard.

Vocation and call have a particular relevance to the season of Lent. The texts set before us this week invite a following of God's call. In Genesis 17, the call to Abram invites a faithful response to a new name, and in that name, a fresh hope. In Romans 4, Paul refers to Abraham and Sarah in order to help the newly forming Christian communities trust in God through faith rather than through their own works. In Mark 8, the call or vocation summons us to follow the way of Jesus in cross-formed discipleship.

Let us open our ears and our lives to the calls we encounter in these words and to the vocations that hearing and following them might evoke in our lives.

A NEW NAME
GENESIS 17:1-7, 15-16

Ancient peoples often gave names to children based on some characteristic of the child or in the relationship to the parent. For example, take the twins Esau and Jacob. These were not family names belonging to grandparents or great-grandparents, nor were they found in those little books you might find in supermarket check-out lines that list hundreds of names for prospective parents to choose from. Esau apparently was a bit hairy and red at birth, for the derivation suggested for *Esau* in Hebrew has something to do with hairy as well as red. Jacob got an even more striking name. Genesis 25:26 speaks of him grasping Esau's heel as he followed his elder brother into life. *Jacob* in Hebrew means something like "he who takes by the heel." Ironically, for much of his early life, Jacob was something of a heel.

In our Old Testament passage for this session, God bestows new names upon Abram and later upon his wife Sarai. Henceforth, they were to be called Abraham and Sarah. The point of this was not to confuse Bible readers who may have thought it was Abraham or Sarah all along. The point of the new names came in the bestowing of new identities upon them.

Consider the context of this story. It had been 24 years since God intruded on Abram's settled life in Haran with the call to a new land (Genesis 12:4; 17:1). It had been 24 years since God promised not only that new land but an heir to the childless couple. Abram then was already 75 years old. A quarter of a decade had now passed, and Abram and Sarai were still on the move and still childless. Well, Sarai was. Abram impregnated one of Sarai's servants, Hagar, to insure there would be an heir. Ishmael had been born, but God had other plans and other promises in mind. To bring those into the light, God decided new names were in order. Abram, which means something like "exalted ancestor," was named Abraham, "father of multitudes." Sarai—still childless and with a 99-year-old husband, things were not looking hopeful—was named Sarah, "princess."

But why? In modern ears, the names may seem more like a gimmick. What's in a name? However, in the life of Israel, and in the promises of God, *everything* is in the name. The new names announced what God was about to do: make a nation out of a centenarian and a princess out of one whom the neighbors no doubt had decided was barren. In the face of such dead ends, God called new life into being, as in Genesis 1, with the sign of bestowing new names.

New names take time to recognize. For an infant, who knows how long it will take to translate those repeated sounds into the expression recognized as self? What about the newly-named Abraham and Sarah? For those who think Scripture is dull, just read a bit further past the end of this passage. God had barely called out the new names before Abraham was rolling on the ground, laughing (Sarah would also laugh later in the story). It is the kind of laughter that arises from "You've got to be kidding!" That is basically what Abraham told God, wishing aloud that God might leave well enough alone and let Ishmael be the future. God did promise to bless Ishmael, but God would be God in terms of the child of promise. Just so Abraham did not forget that, God also determined that the child Sarah would bear would be called Isaac, which means "laughter."

With those new names, God called Abraham and Sarah to trust God. Years before, they honored a calling to follow God by an act of faith. God again invited them to trust in the fulfillment promised in their new names.

Consider your naming in baptism—not simply with your given and family name but with such names as *beloved* and *child of God* and *member of Christ's body*. What are other names you associate with baptism? How do those words shape your identity and who you are called to be?

A RENEWED FAITH
ROMANS 4:13-25

In keeping with his Jewish moorings, Paul in this passage declares Abraham to be the father of us all. "Father Abraham" revealed Judaism's reverence for Abraham. Adam may have been the first human being, and Moses may have been the first prophet; but it is Abraham who is "father." For Paul, faith sets apart Abraham as father and marks those who would call themselves his descendants. It was faith in God's promises, faith that translated trust into action.

The stories of Abraham's faith thread through Genesis 12–24. God directed Abraham to leave country and family and home in order to go to a land not yet identified that God would show him. The invitation came accompanied by other promises involving blessing and descendants. Like the land, however, they remained more on the side of promise than fulfillment. They were promises whose keeping remained in the hands of God. Abraham could do nothing to fulfill them by himself. Indeed, Abraham ran into trouble when he took matters into his own hands. Abraham showed his humanity in these lapses; but on the whole, he exercised faith that trusted God as promise-keeper. Abraham's faith involved not only a disposition of heart and mind but faith that put feet and life into motion. Abraham opened himself to God in faith that took shape first by setting out on a journey. For faith always and inevitably involves movement: movement toward God, movement out into God's world, movement rooted in and directed toward God's promises.

To be children of Abraham invites us to faith. To be children of Abraham invites us to live in hope of the yet-to-be promises of God. As Paul makes clear in Romans, it is faith and not works that accesses those promises and their hope. We do not earn what God offers. We do not take our lives, as persons or communities, and say: "Look at us, God. Give us what we deserve." That is not the nature of promise. You do not promise something to someone who has it in their power to attain it by themselves. Grace is not a shortcut to what we could have done all along. God promises what we cannot do or achieve for ourselves, yet what is necessary for life that is whole and enduring: forgiveness, love, acceptance, justice, mercy, and peace. In trusting such promises, faith engages us on a new journey, a new life.

What makes such newness possible can be heard in a striking affirmation Paul offers in Romans 4:17 (emphasis added): "In the presence of the God in whom he believed, who gives life to the dead and *calls into existence things that do not exist.*" Giving life to the dead is not a new word in the church; we hear it every year at Easter. The problem that individuals and communities of faith sometimes have comes in translating the news of Jesus' resurrection into the promise of how God may bring life to what is dead in our lives, in our institutions, and in our relationships. Maybe that is why Paul goes on to add that God "calls into existence things that do not exist." Think about what Paul proclaims there for a moment. Think about its meaning beyond what God did in the act of Creation at time's beginning, to what God can still do. It is another promise invoking faith.

If God calls into existence things that do not exist, what does that say about the way you conduct your life—in particular the kinds of things you have given up on as hopeless? Obviously, there are some aspects of our lives that deserve that judgment; but what about dreams we have given up? What about hopes we have abandoned? What about promises we have allowed to die? God bears the hope of radical new beginnings.

That same promise, that same affirmation, can challenge persons and the church with enormous possibility and significant risk. We can become used to saying things will never change. We can become used to believing that simply because something has not come to pass in our lifetime that it never will. When Abraham set out on his journey, the promises of God spoke of things that had never been in his life. He already had a home, he already had a family, and he already had a country. Why not sit tight and be satisfied with things as they were even if they were going nowhere? The author of the New Testament Epistle of

Hebrews contemplated that the reason why Abraham and others found motivation to set out on journeys of faith: "They desire a better country, that is, a heavenly one" (Hebrews 11:16). Faith sets its eyes on the promises; it does not stand still and wait for them to come. Faith journeys out.

The God of Abraham brings life from the dead, calling into existence things that do not now exist. In other words, Abraham's God is the God whose promises declare that creation is a work in progress, the future is open, and that individuals and communities of faith need walking shoes more than pew cushions.

Consider the crisis and opportunity that faces those who call themselves Abraham's children today. Judaism, Christianity, and Islam all claim Abraham as father. One promise made to Abraham was that "in you all the families of the earth shall be blessed" (Genesis 12:3). In Jerusalem and the West Bank, in the steppes of Afghanistan, conflicting claims over those ancient promises have spawned violence and acts of terror between Abraham's children that do anything but bless all the earth's families. Extremists in every camp employ the rhetoric of eradicating the infidels. Somehow, somewhere, the children of Abraham need to reclaim family ties before fratricide becomes the order of the day.

How can that happen when conflicts seem so deep and hatreds so intense? If we believe in a God, who, as Paul said, "gives life to the dead and calls into existence things that do not exist," maybe we need to journey out of the isolation of sanctuaries and synagogues and mosques toward one another and toward promises that are God's to give. Perhaps then God would surprise us by resurrecting peace and by calling into existence justice that seems non-existent in cycles of terror that beget retaliation in kind. The journey of faith always begins with single footsteps—with persons willing to trust the future to God, not vengeance. Any takers?

Who serve as the mothers and fathers of your faith? Why? Where do you struggle with trust and faith in God? What hope or insight does Abraham's faith offer you?

A CRUCIAL CHOICE
MARK 8:31-38

"The cross is not and cannot be loved."[1] With those words, Jürgen Moltmann begins *The Crucified God,* his powerful book on the meaning of Christ crucified. At the outset, he dispels any notions of the cross that romanticize or sanitize its reality. The cross is the means by which human beings crucified the Son of God. The cross is the instrument by which suffering and death were inflicted on the innocent servant of God. The cross is first and foremost not a piece of jewelry nor an attractive wall decoration: it is the scandal of how human beings and imperial power treated God incarnate. It was a scandal that was not a surprise, however. Our text today takes up the narrative immediately after Peter's confession of Jesus as the

Christ, the Messiah of God. In this passage, Jesus seeks to make clear the reality of that confession. The Christ he came to be was not the conquering hero and triumphant warrior expected by many. The disciples' expectations about the Messiah unraveled as Jesus' words about suffering and rejection and death flowed out. Such a fate for the Christ of God was totally out of order, and Peter protested.

It may well be that those protests were lodged not merely against the re-formed image of the Messiah that Jesus taught. What of those who, like Peter, had followed Jesus? What did the fate of the Master have to say about the destiny of disciples? That, too, forms a key element of this passage. For even as Jesus introduced what it meant for him to be the expected Messiah, so too did Jesus draw out its implications for the community of believers.

Just as Jesus' teaching of the Messiah was paradoxical to a dominant understanding of that figure, so then did Jesus describe the persons and community who followed the leading of such a Christ described in rather paradoxical terms. Jesus' teaching identifies them as those who would save their life by losing it (Mark 8:35). Likewise, Jesus called disciples to understand that the gaining of the whole world would in fact bring no profit, if in doing so meant forfeiting their life (verse 36). So Jesus assessed the stakes of discipleship, then and now. It is not about survival and profit. Disciples are called to faithfulness in following.

Jesus addressed even more explicitly those who would be followers with three conditions of what that calling entails: (1) Let them deny themselves; (2) let them take up their cross; and (3) let them follow him (verse 34).

The denial of self has often been misinterpreted in the history of the church, confusing it with mental self-deprecation or physical asceticism. The extreme results have on occasion led to a self-hatred that devalues the gift of our God-given life. A more valuable and insightful understanding of the self-denial intended here moves us to consider the sort of self-denial practiced by Jesus. That denial, as pictured in Philippians 2, is the releasing of one's own prerogatives and privileges for the sake of others. Nowhere do the Gospels portray Jesus in a self-punishing, self-hating manner. Frequently, though, the Gospels portray Jesus as one who freely and graciously comes to us as servant and healer.

For us to deny ourselves in the light and example of Christ is to set aside preoccupation with what we deserve (or at least think we do) from others for the sake of what we can offer them. One of the clearest examples of such a selfless attitude may be seen in the life of Albert Schweitzer. Many of us are probably aware of the medical mission work associated with his life. What we sometimes forget is Schweitzer's life before that. As a young man, Schweitzer was considered the foremost organist in Europe. His future as an organ master at any of the great cathedrals was his for the asking. Schweitzer's first book is still 100 years later viewed as a landmark in 20th-century studies of the life of Christ. Schweitzer could have chaired any theological school at a time when such positions held great prestige and prominence. Yet where did Schweitzer spend the greater part of his life? In a small mission hospital in Africa where Schweitzer's clients and patients knew him, not as a keyboard artist nor an imposing theologian, but as a healer with compassion for the least and the humblest.[2]

The point of Schweitzer's life is not that we all buy one-way tickets to the remotest of places and the poorest of persons, though our world is in short supply of those prepared to do just that. Rather the lesson involves learning the gift of setting ourselves out of the limelight in order to participate in the sheer grace of service. When we learn goodness is its own reward, when we discover we do not need to be preoccupied with self to find joy for self, Jesus' invitation to self-denial begins to make sense.

Taking up the cross speaks of the intent and will we exercise when deciding to risk Christian discipleship. In Jesus' time, the Romans required condemned criminals to carry their own crosses to the place of their execution. It was considered to be a final indignity, a cruelty akin to demanding an inmate on death row today to plug in the chair that would be used for his execution. Taking up the cross was not their decision but their sentence. In contrast, Jesus invites the would-be disciple to take up his or her cross, not by coercion but by choice. Just as the denying of oneself must be a freely chosen act, so must the bearing of discipleship's cross be our willing acceptance of the path of servanthood trod first by Jesus.

The cross is a sign of that path as well as its content. Much nonsense nowadays confuses discipleship with anything but a cross. Instead of offering the way of a self-giving Messiah who suffered and died on a cross, too many invitations to faith are strewn with the feel-good promises of material success or instantaneous good health. Jesus' invitation to "take up your cross" is an act of radical trust whereby we acknowledge the path set before us places our reliance on God.

There are crosses to be borne in the keeping of faith. Relating in a mature way with others who constantly patronize or belittle those around them forms one cross-shaped calling of our faith. Forgiving those who continually try that forgiveness, whose holding of old grudges causes them to deny its gift to others, forms a cross-shaped dilemma of our faith. Being gracious in our acceptance of those whose own ungraciousness stands out in their prejudices and stereotyping of others forms a cross-shaped burden of our faith. All are cross-shaped because all were part of the way Jesus ministered selflessly in life and resisted the temptation to strike back with violence against the powers that inflicted death. Jesus exchanged retaliation with mercy in the cross-spoken word of "Father, forgive them; for they do not know what they are doing" (Luke 23:34).

Forgiveness may seem to have outgrown its time or witness, until we see its transformative power, as when an Amish community reached out with forgiveness to the family of a man who killed their children.

Finally, as those who would be followers of Jesus, we are given a third mark upon our identity and calling: We are to *follow* Jesus. For the first disciples, that included a literal walking that followed Jesus' lead, cues, and example. For us today, our Christian walk is likewise informed by the lead and example Jesus provides. We follow this Christ not by mere mimicking of Jesus' way but by aligning our lives according to the qualities of Christ's preaching and coming realm. As followers, we are marked by the humility of knowing ours is not the final say or authority. Followers live by the trust of having one who leads.

Mark offers no clues as to how these words of discipleship were first received as this passage draws to a close. Peter raised no further protest. No misunderstandings were expressed by the other disciples or by the crowd whom Jesus had called to his side for this teaching on discipleship. That silence, in a way, whispers to us to enter into that crowd and wonder, with them, what we would do. Without the comforting circle of friends and fellowship, without the generations of our families before us who have been part of Christian community, with only the invitation of "If any want to become my followers, let them . . . ," what would we have done?

Of course, this is all supposition. We were not there, but we are here. We are here within the familiar surroundings of sanctuary and community, among the comfortable circles of friends and families who have bequeathed to us this tradition called Christian. A final word of caution, however. Following this Christ remains an open invitation and a choice we make every day. If any want to become my followers, Jesus said, let them—let us—deny themselves and take up the cross and follow. We do not come to the identity of being followers of Jesus by inherited birthright or acquired social standing. To follow Jesus comes in the act of following Christ's lead and example and to do so in community with those who share that calling to live by God's grace.

Follow God's call revealed in Christ in order that you may learn what it means to come to the cross.

What calls have led you into faith and into the Christian community? In what ways, and in company with what others, do you discern God's continuing call to follow Jesus? How do you understand and practice self-denial in a positive way that expresses love rather than self-hatred?

---

[1] From *The Crucified God: The Cross of Christ as the Foundation and Criticism of Christian Theology,* by Jürgen Moltmann (Harper & Row, 1974); page 1.
[2] From The Official Homepage for the International Albert Schweitzer Association at *schweitzer.org/english/aseind.htm.*

Community Marks

Scriptures for Lent:
The Third Sunday
Exodus 20:1-17
1 Corinthians 1:18-25
John 2:13-22

What are the marks of the communities to which you belong? That is, what is distinctive about your family, your neighborhood, your workplace, your circle of friends, and your church?

The first 22 years of my life and the past 24 years of my life have been spent in communities marked by strong ethnic identities. In my former years, I was raised in a neighborhood church whose German heritage remained pronounced. While the language in worship was switched from German to English long before my time, every fall brought with it the Wurstmart dinners of homemade sausage and sauerkraut.

In my latter years, I came to serve a small Finnish Congregational United Church of Christ church yoked to a United Methodist congregation; and I stayed in the community after my pastorate ended. Every two years the community of about a thousand people hosts a Finnish-American folk festival that more than triples the valley's population. When I look back at the church community that nurtured me, and the one that brought me to the town I still live in, I see similar markings. Deep-rooted family traditions create strong bonds of caring and a tenacity to maintain those relationships in the face of change. Of course, strong bonds can occasionally be hard to break into as an outsider; and tenacity in the face of change can take on the quality of stubbornness. The markings of any community can function in a way that brings life or resists renewal. How we use the markings of those communities most important to us is critical.

We are called to explore the markings of Christian community as well. What makes us who we are, and what makes us do what we do must fall under the scrutiny and call of God's intentions for community. It is not as if we get to establish all the rules and determine who we will be and what we will do on our own. The season of Lent in particular is a reminder that we journey and function as a community on a peculiar path revealed in the life and ministry of

Jesus. That is not to say we will always agree precisely on what that path will mean in each and every setting of Christ's community. It is to say, however, that the markings of Christian community by definition need to reflect the identity and vocation of Christ. Otherwise, what distinguishes us from any number of fine and worthwhile service clubs?

Lent's invitation to come to the cross is also an invitation to the *community* of the cross, that we might see what marks our journey as the body of Christ. With these passages we now take up that invitation.

COVENANT COMMUNITY
EXODUS 20:1-17

Before we get to the familiar framing of this passage as the Ten Commandments, did you notice the beginning? The passage does not begin with a statement of commandment or handing down of immutable. It begins with a simple affirmation: "Then God spoke all these words" (20:1). Do you remember the first time God spoke in the Bible? Genesis, Chapter 1. When God speaks, creation comes into being. Creation began as an act of God's voicing what life was to become, and it became. Exodus asserts that covenant began in a similar act, with God voicing what life was to become; only now, the voice speaks *how* life is intended to become. Life is intended to be lived in relationship with God and in relationship with one another.

However, before we get to those commanded intentions, Exodus inserts a story between God's voice and God's commands; and the story is all grace. "I am the LORD your God, who brought you out of the land of Egypt, out of the house of slavery" (verse 2). Before we get to the One who issues these commands, we hear again the story of God's gracious deliverance. "I am the LORD your God," God said. The God who calls us into responsible covenant living is the God who, first of all, made living a possibility. Living in freedom meant living with the hope of choosing whether one would serve and obey rather than surviving to do what Pharaoh said. Life in Egypt was all about slavery. Life in covenant is all about living in faithful response to the grace God has shown.

The first four commandments deal with responsible relationship with God and the last six deal with responsible relationship in community with others. Life in Egypt might have allowed the possibility of the former, so long as Israel kept its rituals and theology to itself and did not publicly challenge Pharaoh's claims to divinity. However, one cannot live in responsible relationship with others when slavery is imposed.

Sometimes we Christians get a bit mean-spirited in our attitudes toward our Jewish moorings. "We are grace, and they are law," we rail. Really? Then how does one explain verse 2, where the basis of Sinai's covenant comes engraved on God's gracious deliverance? Or—and this is the curious part— we become downright legalistic when we reduce the commands that follow into a rigid "do-it-or-else" set of rules rather than an invitation to honor and create community as God intends through such actions as these words evoke.

With the story of Exodus fresh in mind and remembrance, the rejection of any god besides the God who delivered Israel from Egypt calls to mind the claims and the fate of Pharaoh. It also stands as a continuing countercultural warning against being seduced by claimants to god-like allegiances or powers. We sometimes take lightly the idea of following idols. Surely we have outgrown such antiquated and primitive understandings. A case could well be made that whatever is the focus of our devotions, and sometimes the altar upon which we lay our judgment and ethics, might well qualify for present-day representations of idols. Individuals, societies, even nations, have a way of worshiping lesser gods that offer great promise or security but come up short in the face of the One who is releasing captives, not making them. Even the sabbath command serves as a stark reminder that no one, not even Pharaoh, can bind Israel or us to ways that bring no rest and thus no life.

The ensuing six commands relate to covenant lived out in human relationships. All but one are stated in the negative, leading some to cast aspersions at "thou shalt nots." Why not be positive? Many reasons have been offered. The one I find most intriguing is this: The fulfilling of human community and relationships in positive ways is almost limitless and, at the same time, reducible to one essential. For if we are to take Jesus at his word regarding the essence of the Law, that one core tenet is love.

How does one love? Again, the ways are almost without number. Even 1 Corinthians 13, with its marvelous imagery of what love is by what love does, does not exhaust the possibilities. However, if the positive keepings of the Law and covenant are summed up in the multitude of love's expressions, the negative statements of Law as "thou shalt nots" underscore the absolute nature that some things are not negotiable. The beginning of that list with *murder* is telling, especially since that word may also be translated as "kill." For those who would easily justify the violence, whether in war or in punishment or in dispute with neighbor, this command dismisses routine appeals to end life. Ethicists and moralists may debate when and where justification for such acts might come, but the command clearly places the onus on those who would seek to prove such validation. The same could be argued on any and all of the following "thou shalt nots."

The marks of community revealed in Exodus 20 are disciplines of covenant, but they are disciplines rooted not in fear of punishment but in awareness of God's gracious acts of redemption.

How would you fill in the open-ended sentence "I am the LORD your God, who . . ."? What have you experienced as God's grace that changes how you live toward God and others?

CROSS-FORMED COMMUNITY
1 CORINTHIANS 1:18-25

Folly is a charge often leveled at anything or anyone out of sync with its time. Sometimes, however, the greatest wisdom in life lies in dispensing with the conventional and setting out on a new and untried path. Perhaps you have heard the old line about the seven last words of a church about to die? *We've never done it that way before.* There have been and always will be those content to let others strike ahead: quick to criticize each misstep of the adventurous but then quick to jump on the bandwagon when all the risks have been taken. So what have folly and wisdom to do with a cross-formed community?

Our passage from First Corinthians explores the dynamics of folly and wisdom in the context of the Corinthian church. As heirs of the likes of Plato and Aristotle, the Greeks in general and the Corinthians in particular were enamored with the tradition of wisdom. Among the traditions of Greek philosophy were several wisdoms about what constituted the divine. The problem was, Paul's preaching directly contradicted at least two of those core ideas.

The mainstream of Greek philosophy had concluded that two qualities were essential for a god to be a god. A god must be impassible, a word related to *passion*, which meant that God could not suffer. A god must be immortal, which meant God could not die. So according to Greek wisdom, a God who suffered and died was a logical impossibility. What did Paul proclaim but Jesus, the Son of God, who suffered and died on a cross? To any person of wisdom in Corinth, a crucified Christ was absolute nonsense. One might as well speak of the earth being round or women being of equal value to men or loving one's enemies or the meek inheriting the earth. It was all just foolishness.

Apparently, though, Paul did not agree. Since the cross permeates his message, Paul needed to state his case for his "illogic." Paul admitted upfront the word of the cross is foolish—but only to those who are weighed down by conventional wisdom. In the wisdom of self-assertion and might-makes-right bravado, the world judged the cross as the ultimate act of folly and weakness. For Paul, however, the crucified Christ was the very power of God for those being saved. Power in weakness, wisdom in folly, God in Jesus crucified—Paul toppled the neat and orderly universe of the Corinthians with the upside-down, topsy-turvy world of a God who brings life through death, a Savior who brings salvation out of crucifixion. The gospel *is* God's folly, no doubt about it. Paul's preaching simply invites one and all to join in holy foolishness.

Paul also acknowledged a crucified Jesus to be a scandal in Judaism. "When someone is convicted of a crime punishable by death and is executed, and you hang him on a tree, his corpse must not remain all night upon the tree; you shall bury him that same day, for anyone hung on a tree is under God's curse" (Deuteronomy 21:22-23). *Anyone* hung on a tree is under God's curse. The cross was scandalized because of the Law's teaching that such a death revealed God's curse on the victim. Only a fool would say otherwise.

A fool like Paul. The gospel of the cross proclaimed the stunning paradox of redemption: The accursed one hung on Calvary's tree was none other than God's Beloved. No one was more scandalized by that idea than Paul himself. As he makes abundantly clear in other passages, no one approached his zeal in persecuting the cross and its followers. However, what had been Paul's stumbling block became his stepping-stone. For Paul the Pharisee, God's folly in Jesus, the crucified and risen Messiah, became his wisdom and then his calling as an apostle.

Paul asserted to the Corinthians that their inclusion in faith's community depended on God's foolishness. "Not many of you were wise by human standards, not many were powerful, not many were of noble birth" (1 Corinthians 1:26). In other words, if God were wise in the ways of this world, Paul informed the Corinthians, they would not be such a motley and diverse crew as they were. God in Christ had gathered into this community a heady mix of the high and low. The Corinthians themselves became Paul's closing argument about the folly of God revealed not only in the cross but in the church God gathers.

That is what makes this passage such a humbling one to transport into our time. Our pews and pulpits are far more like the Corinthian community in composition than they are different. Not many of us are wise according to worldly standards, not many of us are powerful, and not many of us are of noble birth. God's choice of us, like the Corinthians, speaks volumes about God's grace.

That truth has practical spin-offs for our identity and vocation as the community Paul later referred to as the body of Christ (1 Corinthians 12). In the 2,000 or so years of the church's life, members have remarked that some do not deserve our ministry or that some are unworthy of incorporation into our community. In either case, they claim it would not be wise to associate with such people. However, the question naturally arises from this passage in Corinthians: Whose wisdom and whose community are we talking about? Is it the wisdom of what is convenient, what is traditional, what is acceptable? Or is it the wisdom of what is gracious, what is unconditional, what risks the charge of folly for the sake of graciously including others as God has so graciously included us?

We are a cross-formed community, which is to say we are formed by God's grace. That calling comes revealed most clearly in following the One whom the world in all of its wisdom rejected and crucified as unworthy, the One whom the world in all of its power sealed in a tomb so that he would not come back to haunt them. God's folly allowed this to be so that in the weakness of dying the power of rising could be demonstrated.

As God has revealed in the Christ, so God would reveal in those called to be the body of Christ today. For in the cross the foolishness of grace becomes our wisdom. The vulnerability of grace becomes our strength. Grace's inclusion of the otherwise rejected becomes the organizing and outreaching principle of God's community. Why? The cross-formed community finds its life in the foolishness and vulnerability and embrace revealed in the grace of God that is in Christ for us and for all.

In what ways does Paul's understanding of the foolishness of a cross-formed community challenge your life of faith? How might it strengthen your life of faith?

ZEALOUS COMMUNITY
JOHN 2:13-22

The first presidential election campaign to which I paid any real attention happened in 1964. That year the Republicans nominated Barry Goldwater, while the Democrats nominated the incumbent Lyndon Johnson. Goldwater promoted aggressive foreign policy proposals, including the consideration of using nuclear weapons in Vietnam. Johnson countered with charges of zealotry and extremism. I remember a television ad that pictured a little girl picking flowers, and suddenly the image dissolved into the mushroom cloud of an atomic weapon. The clear implication was that a vote for Goldwater meant risking that scenario.

Goldwater, in turn, pulled no punches. In a line that became the hallmark of his campaign, he defended his policies by saying, "Extremism in defense of liberty is no vice."[1] For a 14-year-old growing up in a middle-of-the-road family in a moderate ethnic church in the Midwest, extremism of any sort was suspect. That suspicion must have been shared by a great many others at that time, as the candidate avowing extremism in the defense of liberty lost in the most lopsided election in over 100 years.

I am not prone by personality or conviction to extremism. In racial matters, I am repulsed by extremists who proclaim the message of supremacy. In politics, radicals on the left and the right who know with unyielding certainty what is true and best for everyone else make me nervous. In matters of theology, though, I must confess to a dilemma. There is an unsettling tradition in the biblical witness that fuels the fire of zeal in faith. It is a tradition we encounter in this Gospel passage from John and through this season's journey to the cross.

The setting of John's narrative is the festival of Passover, when masses of pilgrims traveled to Jerusalem and the Temple. Among those who arrived at the Temple were Jesus and his disciples. What they found on arrival in the Temple precincts was a thriving marketplace. Animals suitable for sacrifice were bought and sold. The tables of moneychangers crowded with pilgrims exchanging foreign currencies for the local shekel.

In defense of those sellers and moneychangers, their activities were not only normal but necessary. The laws of Leviticus were quite restrictive regarding what animals could be used. A pilgrim traveling hundreds of miles would be quite encumbered if an animal had to be transported. The sellers of animals provided not only a convenience but a service for pilgrims. In addition, Greek and Roman coins could not be given for the Temple tax paid by the pilgrims. Those coins bore images of pagan deities or Roman emperors. Since the second commandment forbade making any graven images of gods, such coins were forbidden in the Temple. So moneychangers were on hand to exchange the acceptable Syrian shekels for the travelers' currencies.[2]

However, if there were acceptable reasons for the presence of such traders nearby, something was wrong. Perhaps they strayed too close to the more sacred areas of the Temple mount so that their hawking of goods and services drifted into the places reserved for worship. Perhaps they charged excessive prices or exchange rates, taking advantage of religious needs for unfair personal gain. Neither John nor the other Gospel writers identify the specific reason for Jesus' reaction; but react he did, and in an unusually extreme and zealous way.

Words gave way to muscles. Tables tumbled, animals scattered, and coins flew. The one whom some portray as gentle Jesus meek and mild suddenly had a whip in hand. His actions spurred his disciples to recall Psalm 69:9: "Zeal for your house will consume me" (John 2:17). Jesus did act as someone consumed by zeal to defend what he held as sacred from abuse.

In defense of the sacred, the incident at the Temple reveals Jesus to be an extremist ready to risk misunderstanding and censure and even death. When asked for a sign that would justify such drastic action, Jesus made a veiled reference to the cross and resurrection: "Destroy this temple, and in three days I will raise it up" (verse 19). Opponents and disciples heard Jesus' words in the context of the Temple on whose grounds they stood. Misunderstanding is a frequent occurrence in John's Gospel. John says that Jesus was talking about the temple of his body (verse 21). Even though this incident occurred at the outset of John's Gospel, already the cross began to form in the exercise of Jesus' zealous actions.

Zeal may take many forms, as it did in Jesus' ministry. In the Temple courtyard, zeal erupted in the driving out of merchants who made a mockery of a holy place. On the hill of Calvary, zeal unfolded in the agonizing acceptance of undeserved death thereby making a holy place out of a mockery. The cross reveals the extremism of Jesus' obedience and grace. There is no purpose of God too demanding, there is no need of humanity too severe, to which Jesus will not respond. We are only left to wonder, in the words of a hymn often sung in this season, "What Wondrous Love Is This."

What might we learn from Jesus' zeal? Should we disclaim all moderation, tolerance, and compromise and become unyielding extremists at every turn? Absolutely not. While Christ drove out the moneychangers that day, he was also charged with being a friend to tax collectors and sinners. While Jesus did not turn away from the cross when its time came, neither did Jesus inaugurate his ministry by being crucified. Living the life of faith does not mean at each and every moment poising ourselves and our stands on the edge of confrontation and total sacrifice. Life is not a continuing succession of life-or-death crises and choices with no respite between.

Yet such moments of crises and choices do come, moments when our most basic commitments and allegiances are on the line, moments when other gods make claims upon us. It is in those times and choices that faith does become a matter of extremism. It excludes all other claims upon us, save those of the God who has formed and delivered us. In those times, the zealous Christ calls us to obedience, what is needful and faithful to God.

The history of the church is strewn with the wrecks of extremists who confused personal ambition with divine necessity: the Crusades, the genocide of North and South American Indians in the guise of their conversion, the People's Temple of Jim Jones, David Koresh at Waco. Extremism in the name of religion can be as dangerous and hypocritical as any other brand, if not more so, because it invokes the name and authority of God to excuse human barbarity and arrogance.

Yet, the history of the church is also highlighted and illuminated by other extremists whose zeal for unyielding allegiance to God at great personal jeopardy witnesses to the way of Christ. Martin Luther stood before his accusers, refusing to recant his teachings on justification by faith alone. Archbishop Oscar Romero of El Salvador continued to preach and serve among the poor of his country, only to be murdered at the altar of his church as he said Mass.

Such extremists cannot be dismissed nor can their witness to faith's ultimate allegiances. Christ's consuming devotion to serve God and bring salvation to the God-loved world led him to the cross.

Where might it lead us? It may be that such extreme moments come rarely to our lives; but when they do, may we remember who has made and delivered us, who alone merits our zeal. May we remember the cross.

Where have you seen or experienced the positive side of zeal; the negative side? What helps you determine when it is time to take a stand and what risks/costs are worth the price?

---

[1] From the archives of *National Review* at *www.nationalreview.com/flashback/editors200408300851.asp*.
[2] From *The Anchor Bible, The Gospel According to John*, i-xii (Doubleday & Company, Inc., 1966); page 115.

Life Gifts

Scriptures for Lent:
The Fourth Sunday
Numbers 21:4-9
Ephesians 2:1-10
John 3:14-21

What makes life possible? In *Rare Earth,* by Peter Ward and Donald Brownlee, the authors theorize why complex forms of life are likely a rare occurrence in the universe. For example, the parent star (in our case, the sun) has to have a constancy of energy radiating out to heat its planets. Too much or too little heat, and even severe variations in the radiation, and life could not survive. The mass of the home planet would have to be large enough to create a gravitation pull sufficient to maintain an atmosphere, yet not so large as to pull in greater numbers of asteroids that could devastate the planet. These are but the tip of the iceberg for the delicacy of balance in the range of needs for life to exist in an otherwise inhospitable universe.[1]

The question of what makes life possible need not be limited to conjecture on cosmic terms. The question of what makes life possible relates to fundamental needs in our lives. What makes life possible when one thousand or ten million individuals reside in a given area of land that is arbitrarily designated as a social community? What makes it possible there for rights to be respected and needs to be met? How is balance maintained in governance between falling into anarchy or giving in to fascism? To bring this matter down to an even sharper focus, what makes life possible in the intimacy of human relationships, not on the grand scale of societies and cultures, but in the daily interactions within families and among neighbors? What makes the life of a relationship possible when one party does wrong to another, willfully or accidentally? What makes the life of a family possible when disagreements arise and lines are drawn, whether between partners or between children and parents? What makes it possible for us to move forward and grow rather than dwell in accusation or resentment, digging in our heels until nothing and no one moves?

This season of Lent and its journey toward the cross address this issue of what makes life possible. That question grows even larger as the cross nears. Indeed, one could argue that Jesus' teaching throughout his ministry, and in particular when Jerusalem comes into sight, is focused precisely on this matter. What makes life possible when ordinary presumptions of Messiah and followers are turned upside down? What makes life possible as the day approaches when it seems life's possibility will be squelched again under the weight of fearful power exercised in oppression and execution?

What makes life possible in this community called to follow Jesus, not simply in a text-driven journey to the cross through this book but in the ways we practice community and embody Jesus' teachings? The texts for the fourth Sunday in Lent affirm three such prerequisites of life: forgiveness that brings healing, grace that saves, and love that embraces the whole.

THE HEALING
OF FORGIVENESS
NUMBERS 21:4-9

In the German city of Münster, there is a church by the name of St. Lamberti's. It dates back to the 16th century, which is not all that unusual for its locale. What is unusual, however, are three iron cages that hang high on the outside wall of the church's west tower. Radical Anabaptists, ancestors of today's Mennonites, had seized control of the city for a period of time during the Reformation. Catholics and Lutherans persecuted the Anabaptists for their unorthodox theology that

included the tenet of re-baptism. Once the Münster Anabaptists had been ousted from political power, their three main leaders were tortured to death in a public ceremony.

At the conclusion of that spectacle, the torturers threw the bodies of their victims into newly fashioned iron cages and hoisted them to the top of the church tower. There they were left as a warning. The cages were lifted up for all to see, a sight meant to serve as an unavoidable reminder of the consequences of heresy and treason. No one entering that town could miss the gruesome spectacle, nor would it be difficult to learn of its reason.[2] In a time before mass media, that was quite compelling communication. Then again, it might have been equally compelling not to be struck by the rather stunning contradiction of corpse cages hung on the outside of a building consecrated to a crucified Messiah.

"And the LORD said to Moses, 'Make a poisonous serpent, and set it on a pole; and everyone who is bitten shall look at it and live' " (Numbers 21:8). Among the Bible's odd stories, this one ranks high on the baffling list. There was the whining of the people that preceded the disaster. Numbers notes they were "impatient," and impatience leads even the best of us to rash words and actions. They exhibited amnesia, having already forgotten why God brought them out of Egypt. They contradicted themselves, complaining in one breath they had no food or water; and in the next they detested that "miserable food" (manna). So was it no food or bad food? Their answer seems to be "both of the above." Impatience does not pause for the sake of logic or remembrance; it just blurts out what is immediate to the moment: "I want it now." Impatience marked some of the expectations people would later have of Jesus. They wanted kingdom and deliverance now. Such impatience with the cross-formed ways of Jesus may have greased the skids of his rejection.

But back to this odd story of Israel in the wilderness. The peculiar nature of this story is not just Israel's impatience, however. What seems even more unsettling is God's response in the sending of poisonous serpents that killed a number of the complainers. At least, we presume the complainers were the only ones who perished, though the text does not specify that. There may have been innocent victims as well. At least, that is often the way things happen in this world. A rogue nation or a group engages in an action unacceptable to others; and the retaliation that follows ends up with what today we euphemistically call "collateral damage."

This Old Testament story presents a challenge to readers and interpreters. Foremost among those challenges is what we make of God's actions here. In my hearing, the violence attributed to God in this story resembles other passages that attribute orders to put to the sword entire populations of towns and villages, women and children included, to God (for example, Joshua 8:1-26; 10:34-40). Numbers 21, to its credit, does not

try to sanitize this story by saying only the complainers suffered, nor does it give us an easy out by saying that Israel only *thought* God sent the serpents. Scripture does not answer all the questions it sometimes raises.

However, what this passage does affirm connects to the theme for this fourth Sunday in Lent: life gifts. What makes life possible in Numbers 21, even in the face of punishment attributed to God, is God's own providing of a means of healing and forgiveness. Where does forgiveness enter this story? Consider the unusual artifact through which healing comes: a serpent made of bronze. God told Moses that anyone who looked upon this serpent would be healed. To look upon the bronze serpent forced one to look upon what caused the danger, which was not only the bite of a serpent but the complaining brought down this judgment. In other words, looking at the serpent forced one to confront the sin that created the crisis in the first place.

Sin that is not seen and recognized as such lingers. Psalm 32:1-5 relates how sin that is kept inside, silent and unacknowledged, festers and wastes away. Only sin confronted and confessed finds release in the gift of God's forgiveness. The sight of the serpent in Numbers 21 embodies such an understanding and opens to God's forgiveness that brings healing.

Such healing that forgiveness brings is a gift of life. It is surely a gift of life experienced in the intimacy of close human relationships. If one never forgives the partner, the spouse, the child, or the parent, relationship wastes away and dries up. Forgiveness is the gift that makes fresh starts possible. Forgiveness is the gift that renews relationships that might otherwise have careened out of control.

Such healing that forgiveness brings can be a gift of life experienced in the community that calls itself by Christ's name. Without forgiveness, the journey to the cross would dead-end in judgment. Instead, from the cross, Jesus forgave executioners and assured a thief his execution would end not in utter darkness but in Christ's presence in paradise. Without forgiveness, the journey to the cross would point condemning fingers at each and every one who has had times of denial or indifference to Christ. Jesus' forgiveness provides the means for us to resume the way after the detours and stumblings we all make.

What we make of Numbers 21 and its offer of healing forgiveness is left to us. We may choose to hear in this story only the harsh word of God levying judgment. We may choose to hear in this story the gracious offer of God lifting up the means of healing and forgiveness. The choice is important, however, for what we hear tends to be how we then live. Will we hoist up those from whom we are estranged in accusation and condemnation, or will we lift up those same ones with forgiveness in the hopes of healing and reconciliation? May our choice reflect the choices made by Christ encountered on the way to the cross.

When, and how, has impatience led you to bad choices in relationships with others and God? What sights and experiences bring you healing and forgiveness and invite you to offer the same to others?

THE GRACE THAT SAVES
EPHESIANS 2:1-10

Tucked into this session's passage of Ephesians is a verse of enormous consequence in the history of the church: "For by grace you have been saved through faith" (Ephesians 2:8). The central truth that sparked Martin Luther's work was of our being saved or justified by grace through faith. On the surface, this seems a fairly tame statement, not one to raise too many eyebrows. Yet it was a revolutionary idea in Luther's time, and it continues to be in our own. When Johann Tetzel came through Germany selling indulgences, his sales pitch was that a treasury of good works were stored up by the saints. For a contribution to the fund, the benefit of those good works for you or your loved ones—even if they were deceased—could be procured, thereby eliminating time otherwise spent in purgatory. The idea that one's own good works would help one's standing in the eyes of God was powerful enough. Now, however, the sale of indulgences to purchase the good works of others introduced a whole new scheme. Against that, Luther protested that, by God's grace, salvation comes through faith and not works.[3]

That is also the protest we bring to any and all who would argue that God's grace is defined and extended by any other means. It is the protest to be raised when religious extremists of right or left insist on adherence to their particular practices or politics in order to be considered true believers. It is also the protest to be raised when that grace is causally linked to our wallets. When contributions are encouraged through the promise of health or prosperity or a contrived partnership scheme, we are back to the sale of indulgences. God's care and keeping of us, not to mention God's saving of us, is not for sale.

Our salvation by God is a matter of grace accepted by faith. Our works, our actions, and our stewardship are how we respond to God's gracious activity, not how we procure it. Ephesians affirms that we are saved by grace through faith. Let us consider these three core elements.

Through faith. In Greek, unlike English, the word *faith* has a noun form and a verb form. In other words, faith is not simply the content of what we believe or trust; faith is something we do. For that reason, the word *trust* in some ways comes closer to what the New Testament has in mind with the verb form of *faith.* We trust God. *Faith* is a verb because faith engages us in relationship with God; and relationship, whether with God or within families, is always dynamic, expressed in action. Relationship is not merely what you believe about another. Relationship engages that belief and trust with action that gives them substance.

Faith is not in opposition to works as it is sometimes caricatured. Otherwise, why would verse 10 say that God has created us in Christ "for good works"? Active faith is the way we engage in covenant with God.

By grace. The grace of God is what makes that trust not only possible but efficacious. We could trust in God all we wanted to, but it would have no effect if God were not interested in relationship with us. Grace is that interest in God for us. It is grace because it is a gift, an invitation to relationship freely extended. An editor friend by the name of George Donigian once provided me with a definition of *grace* I have been drawn to ever since: Grace is what God consistently does for us that we cannot do for ourselves.

Sometimes the "cannot do for ourselves" has to do with our not meriting or deserving its gift. That is the intersection of grace with human sin, but the "cannot do for ourselves" takes grace beyond the issue of sin alone. Sometimes what we cannot do for ourselves comes from inabilities formed of grief or being at wit's end or being powerless. Those are the intersections of grace with human frailty that may have nothing to do with personal culpability and everything to do with human need. In all those times, we stand in need of the grace of God. So what is the essential action of grace?

Save. While most translations render this verb in verse 8 as "you have been saved," the Greek tense of this verb implies continuing and ongoing action—you *are being* saved. Either way, God's decision action of grace is to save. The latter meaning involving ongoing action simply indicates God's saving is a continuing-all-through-life thing. Why? We are constantly relying on God's grace to save us; and, again, just as grace has to do with more than just sin, so does save. The Greek word *sozo,* translated here as "saved," also carries the meaning of "heal" and "make whole." It is the verb the Gospel writers often employed to describe what Jesus has done in an act of physical healing. So to speak of God's saving is to affirm God acts for the sake of our wholeness, whether wholeness comes by the gift of forgiveness or restoration to relationship or healing.

By grace you are being saved through faith. Faith does not manipulate God to do things for us that God is not interested in doing. Grace already disposes God to act for our good. Trust opens us to that goodness out of needs we cannot meet for ourselves. God has saved us in Jesus Christ. God is saving us every moment of our lives as God's free gift to those fashioned in God's own image to be God's own. Do you believe that? Do you *entrust* your life, your hopes, and your needs to that? That is the invitation we find in this passage of Ephesians: to trust the grace of God to meet the deep and true needs of our lives.

What have been the times and situations where you have experienced God's grace in saving and healing ways? In what ways do you practice faith as a verb?

THE EMBRACE OF LOVE
JOHN 3:14-21

My mother and two older sisters graduated from Beaumont High School in St. Louis. The school was named after Dr. William Beaumont, a native of St. Louis who went on to have an outstanding career as an Army surgeon in the early to mid 1800's. Not only did a grateful city name a high school after the celebrated doctor, the school took as the name of its yearbook *The Caduceus.* Emblazoned on the front of my mother's yearbook from 1928 and at the top of many of its pages is the image of a caduceus. The caduceus is a medical insignia that some of you may have seen before. It is a staff around which wrap two snakes that face each other at the top. In Greek mythology, the caduceus was carried by the god Hermes. The staff is reminiscent of the bronze serpent and its healing power in Numbers 21:4-9.

In John 3:14, Jesus refers directly to Numbers and to Moses lifting the serpent. Jesus did not make this reference in connection to minor or secondary teaching. It served as Jesus' introduction to what many believe is Christ's most concise statement of the gospel: "For God so loved the world that he gave his only Son, so that everyone who believes in him may not perish but may have eternal life" (John 3:16). How many times we have heard that! With the possible exception of the 23rd Psalm, John 3:16 may be the most familiar of all biblical texts. Yet how does Christ begin his teaching of this

COME TO THE CROSS

verse of God's universal and self-giving love? "Just as Moses lifted up the serpent in the wilderness, so must the Son of Man be lifted up" (verse 14).

So what is the correlation between an uplifted serpent and an uplifted Son of Man that paves the way for Jesus' teaching of a God-loved world through the sign of a God-given Child? The serpent and the Son of Man have to do with life. The uplifting of each was for the benefit of those whose eyes might take in a healing and saving sight.

In Numbers, it is said that those who saw the serpent would live. In John, the teaching is that those who believe in the Son will live. The comparison between Moses' life-giving serpent and God's life-giving Son is one in which seeing and believing lead to life. John's remembrance of this connection made by Jesus is not one that is limited to this text either. At the climax of John's Gospel, seeing and believing once again become tied in the story of Thomas. "Have you believed because you have seen me?" Jesus asked. "Blessed are those who have not seen and yet have come to believe!" In the wilderness, it was enough merely to see the serpent to have life. In the case of Jesus, however, seeing is not enough. Whoever believes in the uplifted one is said to have eternal life.

The lifting up of the Son of Man occurred on a hill outside the city walls of Jerusalem. Jesus was uplifted on a staff fashioned of timbers meant to kill, not heal. The uplifting was by executioners seeking to make sure all passers-by knew the consequences of heresy and treason. On the day of Jesus'

crucifixion, it would have been the remarkable eye that could have perceived the love of God uplifted upon it. The cross would make it all seem so contradictory. Prayers for deliverance were answered in crucifixion; hopes for a Messiah now hung in one executed as a common criminal. Looking at the sight of the cross would almost be enough to kill you. It would remind you of all the human folly that had conspired to create such a sight. Yet, was that not what the people of Israel must have seen in the serpent lifted up? In Numbers, to look on the serpent that loomed over them would inevitably remind them of their own complaints that brought down such judgment. They could not see the serpent without seeing themselves.

That is what the cross is partially about. We cannot look upon the cross without seeing our broken-ness from God and one another. Christ lifted up is not the sight we wanted to see, of him or of us. However, it is the sight of God's grace that we need to see, for Jesus lifted up reflects the dramatic embrace of love God offers to the whole world.

What the church is always about, what ministry is always about, is the lifting up of Jesus. Lifting up Jesus reminds us who gets to be Messiah and Savior around here. It is not us. We can and should be faithful servants. We can and should exercise the responsibilities handed into our care, whether by gifts bestowed by the Holy Spirit or offices entrusted by congrega-tional votes; but we are not the final authority for what is right and good. We lift up Jesus.

To lift up Jesus invites us to live, as individuals and communities, in ways that reveal the love of God. For us as disciples, we take our cue for those ways from the life, ministry, love, justice, and compassion of Jesus. We follow the One whose sight, word, and touch restored and continue to restore life and hope. Our calling is to lift up Jesus in our worship, in our service, in the way we interact with one another, and in the witness we bring to this world of God's love in Jesus Christ.

In the third chapter of John, long before the shadows of Golgotha were cast, the uplifted Son of Man is revealed as the sign of God's self-giving love. Jesus is uplifted so that the sight of God's grace for the world may be seen and trusted by all. Jesus is uplifted so that all God's people, all God's creation, might have life. What makes that life possible is God's embrace of the world with love.

Keep your eyes on the One whom God calls us to follow and reveal in our lives, the One whose sight brings us healing and hope, the One who is the incarnate assurance of a God-so-loved-world.

In what ways have you found yourself embraced by God's love? What might a stranger to your community learn of God's love in Christ by the way you live?

---

[1] From a review by Gloria Maxwell of *The Rare Earth,* by Peter Ward and Donald Brownlee at *www.amazon.com/Rare-Earth-Complex-Uncommon-Universe/dp/0387952896.*
[2] From *The Reformation: A Narrative History Related by Contemporary Observers and Participants,* by Hans J. Hillerbrand (Harper & Row, 1966); pages 265-66.
[3] From *Christendom: A Short History of Christianity and Its Impact on Western Civilization,* Vol. II, From the Reformation to the Present, by Roland H. Bainton (Harper Torchbooks, 1964); page 13, and from *A Short History of Christianity,* by Martin E. Marty (The World Publishing Company, 1971); page 210.

Promised Hope

Scriptures for Lent:
The Fifth Sunday
Jeremiah 31:31-34
Hebrews 5:5-10
John 12:20-33

Hope is a curious word. For some, it is practically a synonym for *optimism*. In the words of one old proverb: "Every day in every way things are getting better." Are they? For others, *hope* is a synonym for *wish*: "I hope I get an A on the exam." "I hope the minister finishes the sermon before too long." Is *hope* just another word for what we would like to be true? Genuine hope, biblical hope, involves more than optimism and entails more than wishing. Hope is grounded in what one trusts to be true. Such hope is grounded in the trustworthiness of the ones—and the One—who assert or promise what will come to pass.

As I write this, we are in that season when people vying for votes make all sorts of promises to raise our hopes. Some say we should not believe such promises. I disagree. Making promises is a fundamental ingredient for covenant and community. Making promises and raising hopes is not the problem. Keeping the promises and fulfilling the hopes is the trick. That is why the previous paragraph links hope with the trustworthiness of those who make the promises. If we trust the character of the person making the promise, we will be more apt to accept the promise and look and act toward that hope.

That is one of the reasons why faith and trust are such huge concepts in the biblical witness. The Bible is full of promises. The question is, do we trust them? Do we trust the One who made the promise?

This session's biblical readings bring this issue to our awareness. Jeremiah speaks of God's promise to make a new covenant, one not graven on stone but upon human hearts. Hebrews offers the hope of eternal salvation through the obedience and suffering of Jesus. In the Gospel of John, Jesus offers the hope that out of death can come life. Do we believe these expressions of hope? By *believe*, I do not mean a simple intellectual assent. Such assent is a logical possibility and something I would want to happen. However, on a deeper level, believing entails commitment and action. Do we dare live in a way that acknowledges good and life can come out of even the most dead-end of situations?

God's promises seek to evoke hope beyond what we sing in the hymns or say in the creeds or expect of the pastor on Sunday morning. God's promises seek to permeate our lives and the life of this world with the hope of God's love and justice and compassion.

Hope is not a religious wish list. Hope is to be the blueprint for our activity in this world as those who entrust ourselves to the promises of God. Hope moves us to live and witness and serve based on those promises and not settle for the old worn-out clichés of where the world is headed based on resigned despair or head-in-the-clouds naivete. Hope is faithful living grounded in God's promises. Hope even gives the strength to come to the cross and to see beyond its sorrow and tragedy the seeds of God's gracious purposes and power for life.

A NEW DAY
JEREMIAH 31:31-34

Two days before my wife and I left on vacation one year, I received an invitation to co-lead a writer's workshop. I was asked to fill in for a writer who had dropped out at the last minute, and the workshop would be barely a week after we came back from vacation. I had never led such a workshop in my life. I had no idea how it would work out or if what I would be able to prepare in the

short time available would be of any value to people expecting a workshop with someone else. I had good reasons to say, "Thanks but no thanks. This is not the right time to try something new."

I agreed to do it, however, hoping and trusting that some good would come of this even if that good was "Don't you *ever* do this again!" For if we do not open ourselves to what is new and untried, how will we know what the future might possibly bring beyond repetition of the past or the routines of the present?

"The days are surely coming" (Jeremiah 31:31). These opening words from our reading give an unmistakable clue about where this text intends to take its listeners: into the future. The phrase is a common one in Jeremiah. The words break open the sometimes confining space of the present with God's plans.

At times, the prophets' anticipated day is a disturbing and disrupting one, overturning a present in which people have grown comfortable with injustice and idolatry. But not always. In other times, the people of Israel lived in desperate situations. Faced with imminent threats of invasion and exile, they also knew what it meant to fear the future. In those crises, the prophets offered other words of coming days that encouraged and sustained those who longed for some reason to hope. Keep that context in mind with Jeremiah's text: a context of hope and expectation rather than dread. Perhaps you can identify such a longing for renewed hope and expectation in your own life.

"The days are surely coming, says the LORD, when I will make a new covenant with the house of Israel and the house of Judah" (verse 31). God's promise to Israel through Jeremiah was the gift of a new covenant to the houses of Israel and Judah. In Judaism, *covenant* stood for the relationship between God and God's people. From the "never again" promise to Noah and to creation after the Flood to the choosing of Abram and Sarah, from the deliverance of a nation through exodus and wilderness to the setting apart of a people by the Sinai commandments, God covenanted with Israel.

As Christians, we are heirs to that same tradition. Our relationship with God is a partnership enacted by God's grace and received by faith. Just as it was in the covenants with the children of Israel, covenant binds us with others in relationship to God. Covenant calls us into a community of worship and service, of fellowship and mission, of study and renewal. Covenant asks, "Who will we seek to become together as a community faithful to Jesus Christ?"

When Jeremiah looked forward to the new covenant that God would create with Israel, several characteristics emerged. The first one is "I will put my law within them, and I will write it on their hearts" (verse 33). The Sinai covenant relied on external signs of what God's covenant required: commandments etched in stone, an ark built to exact specifications, sacrifices spelled out in great detail. In the days to come, however, Jeremiah wrote that the guiding principle of God's Torah would be engraved within the human heart.

Covenant insists community can never be satisfied with judgments or standards that are purely external. Conservative or liberal, evangelical or mainline, the usual labels used to sort people as "in" or "out" of church or salvation fall sadly short of the covenant God writes on the human heart.

Jeremiah's next characteristic of the new covenant is actually nothing new at all: "I will be their God, and they shall be my people" (verse 33). We see the same idea in Psalm 100: "Know that the LORD is God. / It is he that made us, and we are his" (verse 3). God chooses to be our God: a choice made in our creation, a choice confirmed in our redemption. Part of faith accepts God's choice to be joined in covenant to us, just as part of faith also accepts our standing in that relationship: We are the people of God.

To be the people of God means, among other things, there is not one person in the faith community who is unimportant to the whole body. We need to value everyone's presence and gifts. We need to identify and cultivate those gifts in one another in the same way that God does. Each one in the community has been led there by God. On the flip side, to be the people of God means that no persons in the congregation are more important than the whole body. No person should speak or act in the God-role for all the others. Humility goes a long way in leadership. Maybe that is why Jesus once told the disciples that those who would be great must be those who are servants to all (Matthew 20:26; Mark 10:43). Leadership in the church is not a matter of waving the flag of one person's importance.

All of us—ordained and laity, long-time members and newcomers to community—live on the human side of Jeremiah's assertion: "I will be their God, and they shall be my people" (Jeremiah 31:33). We all have roles to play, we all have gifts to share, and we all have opinions that at times differ from others. However, those roles and gifts and opinions are intended by God to build us up as a covenant community, not divide us into factions. For the basic identity of our faith communities resides in our individual differences and in the common calling to be the people of God.

Another characteristic of the new covenant comes in the declaration of where and how people will come to know God. "No longer shall they teach one another, or say to each other 'Know the LORD,' for they shall all know me, from the least of them to the greatest" (verse 34). Knowledge of God, or faith, is not merely to what we have received from others, no matter how doctrinally correct or precisely stated. Knowledge of God will come from within. Jeremiah's words do not reject the role of teaching or preaching in the covenant community. However, interpretation and proclamation do not substitute for the experience of grace. At some point, the one who seeks covenant with God must find personal connection with that covenant's place in her or his life.

In Jeremiah's new covenant, as in Christ's, the fundamental experience of God's work is forgiveness. "For I will forgive their iniquity, and remember their sin no more" (verse 34). Think of that—not only in terms of what it reveals of God but what it reveals of God's people and of the covenant community of which you are a part. If forgiveness is the primary way we know God, can forgiveness be far behind in what identifies the heart of Christian community? In the Lord's Prayer, Jesus taught that forgiveness is not just the gift we seek from God but the gift we offer to each other (Matthew 6:9-15).

Jeremiah's words bring life and hope to the days ahead. They remind us, as individuals and communities of faith, that the future is a place of promise and new covenant. A covenant engraved on our hearts, a covenant binding us together, a covenant laden with God's forgiveness of us and evoking our forgiveness one of another.

Is the future a place of hope or foreboding for you? Why? In what ways do your actions embody hope and forgiveness?

A MELCHIZEDEK PRIEST
HEBREWS 5:5-10

Hebrews 5:5-10 is actually the second half of a larger section that explores Jesus as High Priest. Some of the language and imagery may be difficult to follow today. Our religious experience does not include a system of worship using animal sacrifice as was the case with Judaism while the Temple stood. The high priest then served as the closest figure to a mediator between God and the people. Only the high priest had access to the holy of holies in the Temple, where the presence of God was thought to be. That holiest of places was entered only once a year on the Day of Atonement, when a series of sacrificial rituals led by the high priest cleansed the sanctuary (including the inner sanctum or holy of holies) and the people.

The other part of this text that makes understanding difficult is the reference to Jesus as a high priest "according to the order of Melchizedek" (verses 6, 10). The phrase itself comes from Psalm 110:4, which was quoted earlier in Hebrews 1:13. The psalm itself is a royal psalm, and in the first chapter of Hebrews it is used to assert Jesus' superiority over the angels. Here, however, the psalm focuses on the mysterious Melchizedek. Who was this?

In Genesis 14:18, Melchizedek is the king of Salem who blesses Abram with a sacrifice of bread and wine. Many hold *Salem* to be another name for *Jerusalem.* As a result, the interpretation suggests that since the act of blessing is often done by one in a superior position, then one who blessed Abram must be superior. The seventh chapter of Hebrews follows this line of interpretation in great detail.

However, the question to be asked of the text on this fifth Sunday of Lent is, What has a priest after the order of Melchizedek to do with the promised hope brought to us in God by Jesus? One response has to do with how the whole of Hebrews 4:14–5:10 portrays the high priesthood of Jesus. The passage confesses Jesus, like all other high priests (and ministers, to broaden the implication) to be human. Yet, unlike all other priests and ministers and writers and readers of lectionary studies, Jesus was without sin. While the high priests of the Temple had to make sacrifice for their own sin as well as that of the people served, Jesus did not. The sacrifice Jesus offered as high priest was himself, and it is effective for eternity. Our hope is based on the perfect sacrifice of Jesus as high priest, an act that reveals God's love and grace through the cross and an act that gives us eternal access to God. "Having been made perfect, he became the source of eternal salvation" (Hebrews 5:9).

One other important point this passage brings to our understanding of hope is this: Jesus "offered up prayers and supplications, with loud cries and tears . . . and he was heard because of his reverent submission" (5:7). Many interpreters connect this offering up of prayers and supplications with Jesus' prayer in Gethsemane. Jesus also prayed on the cross. Jesus prayed for the forgiveness of enemies. Jesus prayed the lament of being forsaken by God. Jesus prayed for God to receive his spirit. Hebrews says, "He was heard." Yet Jesus died on the cross. What possible hope do we see there? Sometimes, in the midst of experiences of crisis and trouble and pain, we take those experiences as suggesting God's indifference, abandonment, or perhaps even punishment. The experience of the cross, in and of itself, could surely be taken in those ways, as they were by those who ridiculed Jesus. However, Hebrews affirms that "he was heard." Jesus was heard, not by a miraculous escape but by resurrection.

The hope we are promised in God is not always according to our timetables. The hope we are promised of God may well even go beyond the horizons of this earthly life, but that does not mean we are consigned to despair. That does not mean death has the final word. God has the final word, and that word is not the word of death and suffering but the word of resurrection and new life.

Can we trust that word? That is why we call this venture faith. That is why Hebrews will later affirm, "Now faith is the assurance of things hoped for, the conviction of things not seen" (11:1). Our promised hope is that even in our Gethsemane and Golgotha times, God hears. God will not forget. God is the God of resurrection for Jesus and for us.

How do you understand the significance of depicting Jesus as a high priest? When and how have you been able to trust that God hears even when it does not seem to be so?

A FRUITFUL GLORIFICATION
JOHN 12:20-33

Several years ago we traveled to Germany to visit our former exchange student and his family.

During our visit we took a two-day excursion to Innsbruck, Austria, where we visited a small restaurant. The front room was full, so the waitress took us to a large back room. Above the table where she seated us, we noticed a large wooden crucifix on the wall. This was not surprising in a region where crosses in public places and on mountaintops were fairly common.

What was unusual about this crucifix was that tied to the feet of Jesus were several ears of corn. Perhaps the restaurant owner simply wanted to add a bit of décor; or maybe the ears of corn represented an offering of sorts, a vestige of some ancient practice of attaching a remnant of last year's harvest to an icon to insure a good harvest in the coming year. This was March, after all. Then again, this was also the season of Lent. In my eyes and heart, the ears of corn on the crucifix resonated with a verse that is part of today's Gospel lesson: "Very truly, I tell you, unless a grain of wheat falls into the earth and dies, it remains just a single grain; but if it dies, it bears much fruit" (John 12:24).

John's passage is set in Jerusalem in the days preceding the Passover festival. That festival commemorates God's deliverance of Israel from Egypt when the Hebrews were instructed to smear the blood of sacrificed lambs over their doorposts. According to the story in Exodus, when the angel of death descended, those homes so marked were "passed over" while those without it suffered the loss of their first-born sons. Many Jews made a pilgrimage to Jerusalem to celebrate Passover. According to the ritual, on the eve of Passover a lamb would be sacrificed at the Temple to commemorate God's deliverance from slavery in Egypt.

Connecting the feast of Passover to Jesus' impending hour is far more than a coincidence of calendar dates for John. In the opening chapter, when John sees Jesus walking toward him, he says, "Here is the Lamb of God who takes away the sin of the world!" (John 1:29). The next day, John repeated the phrase: "Look, here is the Lamb of God!" Before Jesus did anything at all in this Gospel, his coming was linked with the sacrificial lamb. The description of the Crucifixion in John 19 says that Jesus' legs were not broken, which was common in this form of execution. John 19:36 says, "These things occurred so that the scripture might be fulfilled, 'None of his bones shall be broken.'" This may refer to the description of celebrating the Passover in Exodus 12:46, thus making a further connection between Jesus and the Passover lamb.

Jesus told the disciples, "The hour has come for the Son of Man to be glorified" (John 12:23). The time has come. The future is now. This is the hour of glorification, but what does it mean to be glorified? In the Old Testament, the glory of God is not exclusively what makes God different from us. Rather, God's glory is how and when God reveals God's own self and power and presence. Thus in Exodus 40:34-38, the glory of God that fills the Tabernacle is linked to the cloud that led the people of Israel through the wilderness by day. Once the people of Israel left Egypt and entered the wilderness, they continued to require God's

help and leading. When manna was to be given, Moses and Aaron spoke about that gift of God's providence by saying, "In the morning you shall see the glory of the Lord" (Exodus 16:7). The glory of God in Exodus is associated with God's choosing to act in ways that give life to those pilgrims.

This passage from John opens with pilgrims who had come to Jerusalem to observe the Passover. They also desired to see Jesus. When Jesus was informed of their seeking him, he spoke of God's glory. How would this act of glorification, of God's acting for the sake of life, come about? Jesus answered, "Unless a grain of wheat falls into the earth and dies, it remains just a single grain; but if it dies, it bears much fruit. Those who love their life lose it, and those who hate their life in this world will keep it for eternal life" (John 12:24-25).

Jesus taught that God's glory will come in the seeming contradiction of death giving birth to life. The words have a counterintuitive edge to them, as does the deliverance and the discipleship to which they point. Glorification, God's acting on behalf of and for the sake of life, will be preceded by death and burial. Discipleship in the light of such glory is not clinging to life but holding on to hope.

Having announced the arrival of this hour and having taught its meaning in the figures of a grain of wheat, Jesus said about this moment, "Now my soul is troubled" (verse 27). Yet, this hour also reveals trust. Jesus recognized that this hour has been the reason for all his hours. Yet, Jesus' trust is that through all the suffering that he would endure, what was about to happen was God's glorification. The promised hope of God's glorification was enough for Jesus, so Jesus said, "Father, glorify your name!" (verse 28).

In the stillness left as those words dissipate and a cross comes into view, the question is, Is the promised hope of God's glorification enough for us?

When have you seen or experienced the paradox of life emerging out of death? What "grains of wheat" in your life and in your congregation might need burial in order for new life to spring forth and bear fruit?

assionate Trust

Scriptures for Lent: Palm and Passion Sunday

Isaiah 50:4-9a
Philippians 2:5-11
Mark 14–15

In the grade schools I attended in St. Louis, a parade always marked the end of the school year. The local drum-and-bugle corps dressed up in satin shirts and slacks. The lower grades crafted banners from wood, coat hangers, and crepe paper. Parents and grandparents and neighbors lined the streets around the school to see all the children, listen to the music, and watch the banners fluttering and sometimes disintegrating in the breeze. After marching around the school for a few blocks, we would return to the playground so the buses could take us to Chain of Rocks Park for a picnic. The parade itself, as parades are apt to do, actually went nowhere.

That is, after all, what distinguishes a parade from a procession. A parade does not need a destination. It simply draws attention to itself for the moment, and then it is over. A procession, on the other hand, has a definite goal to which the movement leads. Occasionally at those grade schools I attended, we would also see processions. Long lines of cars drove by with headlights on in broad daylight, proceeding from a mortuary or a church to a nearby cemetery named Calvary.

This Sunday is designated Palm Sunday and Passion Sunday. Palm Sunday observances sometimes take on the characteristic of parades. We delight in the presence of children. We enjoy the music. We might even march into the sanctuary with exotic fronds imported just for the event. If that is where we leave it, the parade of palms may—like other parades—not take us anywhere. Imagine someone totally unfamiliar with the story of Jesus attending such a Palm Sunday service and then an Easter service. They might be left to wonder, *What happened?* How did we get from the Jesus "to whom the lips of children made sweet hosannas ring" to the Jesus against whom "the powers of death have done their worst, but Christ their legions hath dispersed," the Jesus who "fought the fight, the battle won"? What powers? What fight? Wasn't everybody happy last Sunday at the parade?

Except that Palm Sunday was not a parade that went nowhere. Palm Sunday was a procession that led into the events of Passion Week. Like those processions my schoolmates and I watched that headed to a cemetery named Calvary, so did the procession into Jerusalem over the course of the next days lead to a killing hill named Calvary.

The biblical texts for today trace the course of the procession that Jesus walked to Calvary. *Passion* has sometimes been heard as a synonym for overheated desire of the sort typically exploited by writers of steamy romance novels. Forget that meaning. Elsewhere *passion* can mean something that we so love and are committed to that we are willing to sacrifice for its achievement. Keep that meaning in mind; but add to it what the language of the New Testament reveals, for the word we translate "passion" most closely means "suffering."

Jesus entered Jerusalem with remarkable trust—trust willing to endure suffering, trust prepared to seek good for others even when it would bring hardship to him. This chapter speaks of such trust as "passionate." It does so from the understanding of passion as suffering (and suffering does come for Jesus) and from Jesus' earnest commitment to act in faith and trust God's purposes—come what may. Hear then these stories of Passion that form the procession route as we come to the cross.

STANDING FIRM
ISAIAH 50:4-9a

To rightly hear Isaiah among these passages of palms and passion, step back for a moment from the entry of Jesus into Jerusalem.

Isaiah's voice does not speak from just outside the city walls where "Hosanna!" will soon be shouted. Isaiah's voice called out when Jerusalem's walls lay crumbled and destroyed. Isaiah's voice cried out when Jerusalem itself was for an increasingly smaller number a distant memory and for the great majority an open question about the future. Isaiah's voice spoke in the midst of Israel's exile in Babylon, whose armies had destroyed the city and the hopes once thought to be impregnable.

The writings of Second Isaiah (Chapter 40 onward) address the crisis of exile. As such, they bring to this day a much earlier experience of passion and suffering—except for them, the suffering stretched behind and around them. They need not have looked forward like the disciples of Jesus, wondering what all this talk of passion would lead to. Second Isaiah's community consisted of those who were led away into captivity years and decades past. Passion and suffering marked their past and permeated their present. At least, it did for those who still carried the longing for Jerusalem.

Many of the exiles apparently had either settled in or resigned themselves to life in Babylon. The words of Isaiah were intended to invigorate those who still carried hopes of re-entry to Jerusalem and to stir up those who had become accustomed to their captivity and captors. Who knew what awaited them in a home they had not seen or known for decades?

Isaiah presumed to know. In today's passage in particular, Isaiah brought to Israel's attention affirmations of how God prepares this new way ahead. Each affirmation acknowledges what "the Lord GOD" does: gives the tongue of a teacher, opens the ear, and helps.

Who is the servant of God whom God so helps? The issue is not resolved. Several other passages in Second Isaiah along with this one are sometimes referred to as the Servant Songs (see also 42:1-4; 49:1-6; 50:4-9; 52:13–53:12). Some believe the servant to be Israel, called to renewed service and mission out of the experience of exile. Others hear the songs in reference to a particular individual who works in those circumstances.

From the time of the early church, these songs have also been seen through the prism of Jesus' ministry. The last of the servant songs in Isaiah details the suffering of this servant in ways that reflect Jesus' Passion. To hear the message Isaiah gave to the people in exile enhances whatever connections we may find with the life and work of Jesus, for Jesus lived and ministered within his Jewish traditions.

Isaiah 50:4-9 offers the imagery of a servant who is resolute in the face of trial. Again, that resoluteness of character does not originate in the servant but in the way that God makes possible. The opening verse affirms how God has "given me the tongue of a teacher." In the context of Isaiah's community, the work of God's servant to stir hope would have required extraordinary eloquence given the stark realities of that situation. They were a people held captive. Their home and capital lay in ruins hundreds of miles away across inhospitable landscapes. The teaching of hope would have been a challenge. Sometimes we forget that Jesus' final week in Jerusalem, at least until his arrest, was a time of extensive teaching. With the crowds at the Temple, with the disciples apart, Jesus filled his final days with teaching.

God also acted to open the ear of the servant in Isaiah 50:5. It is hard to know what to speak when one never listens. Attentiveness to God and attentiveness to those addressed form important components of this God-strengthened discipline. I suspect we often hear this affirmation of Jesus primarily in terms of his silence in trial, especially given the description in verse 6, which evokes for Christians the beating that Jesus endured. Yet I also hear this word of God opening the ear of the servant as deeply important in Jesus' ministry. Jesus did listen. He engaged in conversations that respected and commended the views of others. In the garden of Gethsemane, the prayer of Jesus no doubt engaged in deep listening as he wrestled with the cup before him.

Verses 7 and 9 affirm, "The Lord GOD helps me." God as the helper of Israel had been a long-standing trust in Judaism. Would God still help even in the Exile? Isaiah answered in the affirmative. Notice, though, it was not an answer that removed all difficulty and obstacles. There was contention. There were adversaries. Shame and disgrace and guilt were all mentioned; but in the end, God's help would be sufficient. The journey from Babylon to Jerusalem would be no cakewalk, physically or spiritually; but it would be possible because of God's help.

As Christians view Passion Week through the lens of Isaiah's words, the experiences seem to contradict trust in God's help. Jesus experienced trumped-up charges and curious trials, the ridicule of a crown of thorns, the shame and suffering of a body stripped for flogging. Religious and political authorities conveniently settled for guilt. Gossips beneath the cross belittled the notion of God's help by saying that the crucified one, if he was who he said he was, could call down an army of angels.

For Jesus, however, God's help did not consist of parlor tricks or military intervention. God's help was to be trusted, even in the face of death. Jesus set his face like flint toward Jerusalem, come what may and knowing all too well what would come. "It is the Lord GOD who helps me." The words are Isaiah's. Jesus demonstrated them in his trust. This week invites us to ask, Are those words and that trust ours as well—come what may?

In what ways have you experienced God's help in times of conflict and suffering? Where might God be helping you to stand firm at this moment?

CHRIST-MINDED
PHILIPPIANS 2:5-11

A hospital near my community observes an annual Pastoral Care Week. On one of its days they host local clergy for a luncheon and a program. I recall one year's program on organ donation. Organ transplants have become a fascinating component of modern medical technology. Hearts, kidneys, corneas, livers, skin, bone, cartilage—all can be given to extend and enrich life. Their basic limitation, with the exception of some kidney transplants, is that the donor must be deceased. Decisions have to be made quickly, and conditions have to be right for transplants to be possible. There is no technology whereby one person's heart or liver can support two bodies simultaneously. With transplants, an organ once in one body now resides in another. The old organ is gone. Organ recipients do not walk around with two hearts or two livers. Organ transplants can be done but not organ sharing.

Or can it? One of the organs that medicine has yet to transplant is the human brain. I am not aware of anyone or any group seriously working on the mechanics of such a transplant. Too much still needs to be learned about the brain's mysteries, especially its functions that link it with the human mind. Yet what does Paul write in Philippians 2:5? "Let the same mind be in you that was in Christ Jesus." So how can another mind be in us?

A friend once told me of a conversation she had with a man after a worship and prayer service both had attended. Her acquaintance was a highly educated person, an engineer at McDonnell Douglas, working in the space program. Their conversation touched on how he balanced the emotional and sometimes fundamentalist bent of his church with the highly abstract and scientific world in which he worked. His answer? When he goes to church, he said, he "lays his mind at the altar."

Perhaps he did not intend it that way, but his answer strikes me as too easy and too dangerous. Just how does a person purge one's mind for worship and then pick it up again when it is time to return to job and home? If his mind stands between him and God during worship, wouldn't it do the same during the other hours of his life? Laying the mind at the altar is a bit too risky for me, for who knows if you will remember to pick it up on your way out!

I say that half in jest and half in fear, for how many *do* leave their minds at the altar only to fall prey to spiritual manipulators? How many minds were left at the altar when Jim Jones presided over his community's mass suicide? How many minds get left at the altar when we subjugate our God-given reason to those who presumptuously claim the mind of Christ for their own self-asserting authority? History is littered with the wrecks of minds left behind in emotional, religious, and political stampedes.

Having the mind of Christ, in my judgment, is a matter of our mind's co-existence with that of Christ's. We daily and continually seek to conform and instruct our minds by the mind of Christ. The mind of Christ is not just for individuals; it binds together the community of faith. So the question becomes, What attitudes and actions would give witness to Christ's mind functioning among us? What might having such a mind bring to this day when we consider Jesus' passionate trust as he entered Jerusalem?

As the verses of Philippians 2 unfold, the mind of Christ turns us to rejecting privileged standing for the sake of service. The mind of Christ does not claim prerogatives by virtue of God's grace and love but humbly employs those gifts in words and actions of obedience. As Jesus entered Jerusalem, he did not force acceptance of his way. As noted in the earlier comments on Isaiah, Jesus stood firm in his trust in God and his resolve to do God's will. Nowhere did Jesus impose that trust or that will on others. His listeners needed to make their own decision to trust. Having the mind of Christ among us forces us to discern the difference between privilege and leadership, which sometimes seem hard to separate even in the community that bears Christ's name. Old habits and old mindsets can be hard to break.

The mind of Christ is not one marked by lockstep and unthinking obedience. The mind of Christ freely takes on the yoke of service and trusts God not out of duty but out of love. Though equal to God, Jesus came among us as a servant. In the Gospel of John's record of Jesus' Passion, Jesus washed the feet of the disciples, which was an extraordinary act of humility that embodied his servant ministry (John 13). Having the mind of Christ among us pushes us to consider our own calling to servanthood. How and where do we engage the mind of Christ in such humble service? To put it another way, whose feet might we end up washing if we were more Christ-minded?

Even though Jesus possessed God's eternal nature, Jesus submitted himself in trusting obedience even though it would mean death on a cross. Having the mind of Christ among us challenges the community of faith to remember that individual or institutional survival is not the primary goal of a follower or a community of Jesus. Faith takes shape in expending our lives in Christ's service, trusting that it will be God—not our own devices, not even our own long histories—who will bring new life and renewal into being.

Having the mind of Christ does not always co-exist easily with conventional thinking about power and humility. It might be argued that the crowds turned against Jesus because he did not reflect their thinking about the Messiah, about power, about leaving service to the servants, and about taking whatever advantage and privilege whenever possible. It also might be argued that to be Christ-minded in such ways as Philippians speaks of will not be an especially popular or appealing strategy today. So the question is, Who do we believe? Whose mind guides our decisions and priorities? "Let the same mind be in you that was in Christ Jesus."

What does having the mind of Christ mean to you as you continue to grow in faith and service? What new thoughts and commitments might the mind of Christ bring to you?

BROKEN AND POURED OUT
MARK 14–15

Some stories are gripping because we have no idea where they are leading or what will become of their chief characters. Many enjoy the works of O'Henry precisely because of the twists that come at the end that catch us by surprise and leave us wondering why we did not see them coming. Other stories are gripping because we know exactly where they are leading. We may have read or heard them many times before; but once the drama begins, we are caught up in its flow. Perhaps we do at times wonder, and hope, for a different outcome.

The Passion narrative may be one such story for you. Depending on how long you have been involved in Christian community, you may have heard it, or at least parts of it, year in and year out. Each of the Gospel writers approached it from slightly different angles, offering varying insights to words spoken and actions taken. Yet they all converged to weave a single narrative: An innocent victim is killed by the warped intentions of some religious leaders abetted by political power that has exchanged justice for fear-driven convenience.

I say "warped" in the previous sentence purposefully even as I choose to say "some religious leaders" versus a categoric smear of Judaism. Why? No religious tradition holds the corner market on losing sight of principles. Just about any religious tradition I am aware of has had moments when adherents and leaders twisted the definition of good for self-serving purposes. The narration of the trial in Mark 14:53-65, with a few changes in names and charges, would fit quite nicely into the narrative of the Inquisition under Torquemada in "Christian" Europe. Then there is the trial before Pilate where it seems Pilate wished to do the right thing but was compelled by the court of popular opinion to do otherwise. It would not be the first, and by far the last, time when political expediency had settled for scapegoats rather than truth.

Why do we tell this narrative year in and year out when so many of us have heard it so often? Because it tells truths that must be remembered if we are to come to the cross with eyes and spirits wide open.

Verses 22-25, which we know as the institution of the Lord's Supper, foreshadow the events of the unfolding plot. Jesus lifted up broken bread and told the disciples that it was his broken body. Then he lifted the cup filled with wine and told them it was his blood, the blood of a covenant "poured out for many." He enriched the message of God's salvation and liberation with a new level of meaning.

As the story continues we hear truths that may make us uncomfortable. One is the truth that even the boldest in faith is not immune to weakness. The threads of Peter's story, beginning with his assertive "even though all become deserters, I will not" (14:29) through the boast of dying with Jesus before denying him and continuing to fearful replies, reads like a train wreck in slow motion (Matthew 26:30-35; Mark 14:26-31; Luke 22:31-34; John 13:36-38). Bravado is not what makes it possible to stand before the cross.

Other such truths weigh in when Jesus entered a garden in order to pray. He asked Peter, James, and John to accompany him as he went apart for a time of prayer. These three had formed the unofficial core of leadership among the Twelve. They had been among the first of the disciples called (Mark 1:16-20). They had accompanied Jesus into the house of Jairus when Jesus raised the official's little girl from death (5:37-42). Jesus had taken these three up to a mountain where he was transfigured (9:2-9).

However, when those who had seen Jesus raise a girl from death and experienced the glory of transfiguration were asked to keep vigil while Jesus prayed, they slept. They fell asleep not once, not twice, but three times. Jesus had carried them and encouraged them during his ministry; but at a time when they might provide such support, they did not. Perhaps the drowsiness can be attributed to the late hour or the multiple glasses of wine involved in a Passover observance. Might the story also not be telling the truth that it is fine for us to be supported in faith by community, by those we look up to? Sometimes, though, when we are called upon for support in order to do ministry, we fail. Faith that is all take and no give is sleep and avoidance. So when the garden story ends with the disciples fleeing into the night, we are not surprised. Faith that avoids hard times and disciplines is not the faith that makes it possible to stand before the cross.

What faith makes it possible to come to the cross? Part of such faith, tucked away at the end of the account, might be overlooked. For while the disciples all fled, others remained at a distance: the women who followed Jesus, the women who provided for his Galilean ministry. These women provided the first hopeful sign in this awful account that Jesus' words of trust and relationship had borne fruit. They were there at the crucifixion of our Lord.

In the garden and upon the cross, Jesus engaged God in prayer. In the garden, it was prayer that earnestly sought another scenario than the one that seemed to be unfolding. On the cross, Jesus raised the prayer of the psalmist in Psalm 22 of the experience of God-forsakenness. Some may shy away from such words, thinking them disrespectful. Jesus boldly offered them in prayer as an act of faith. Lament expressed trust in God's openness to hear the truth of our lives. There was a subtle connection between prayer for the removal of this hour and the experience of being forsaken by God, and that connection was a deep trust that God would hear. Jesus also prayed in the garden that God's will be done. Psalm 22 ends with expressions of praise and trust in God.

Broken and poured out: at the table, on the cross, Jesus enacted those words with his life, for our life. Why? So that our broken lives, our poured-out hopes, might find possibility of gracious renewal.

What parts of this story do you find most compelling; most bewildering; and above all, most truth-telling about your life? What do you hope this story will offer you as you come to the cross this week?

Easter Days

Scriptures for Easter:
Isaiah 25:6-9
1 Corinthians 15:1-11
John 20:1-20

Easter and Christmas form the two chief festivals of the church year. Both are preceded by periods of preparation, but the similarities soon disappear.

Christmas can attract us with the sentimentality of a tiny babe, lullabied by the soft sounds of stabled animals and a mother's song. It is a pleasant picture, comfortably envisioned from experiences or ideals surrounding new birth. Easter, on the other hand, flies in the face of experience. We all *know* that death is final in this world. Delayed, yes; cheated, perhaps; but no human being can claim immunity from it. All of our personal experience and thousands of years of human history point to one inescapable conclusion. Death is certain. In the face of the certainty of death, we hear the proclamation of Jesus' resurrection.

Easter forms the starting point for Christian faith and hope. Forget for a moment the teachings of Jesus, the miracles, and the healings. Set aside the birth stories and the parables and the Sermon on the Mount. The writers of the Gospels and Epistles all wrote and remembered looking back through the prism of Jesus' resurrection from death. Jesus' resurrection became the vantage point from which all the other stories came to have enduring significance beyond literary or theological curiosity. Likewise for us, the story proclaimed on Easter morning serves as a vantage point from which to scan the whole of our lives—past and future.

The perspective offered by that vantage point is stunning to the point of incredibility. Where once we could see before us only that insurmountable ridge called death, Easter beckons to an entirely new and unexplored vista. We still can look back from its height upon the path that has led here: the winding road leading to Jerusalem and a cross, the twisting paths upon which you and I still travel in faith. However, from Easter's emptied tomb we can stand on tiptoe and catch a glimpse of hope's panorama.

All of which is fine, except for one thing: Do you believe it?

Which is to say, do you believe Easter's story of God raising Jesus? This is not a story of resuscitation, of a heart restarted after cardiac arrest. This is not the story of Lazarus, revived after three days in the tomb only to die again. Easter claims the story of a Jew named Jesus entering death's door and coming out transformed, risen, on the other side. Do you believe that?

Our coming to the cross has brought us now to Easter Day or more accurately, Easter *days*. Easter is not simply a singular day in the church's year. Easter days form the calendar for every day that we live, work, hope, and serve in the light of Easter's news. "Christ is risen!" is more than a liturgical greeting; it is the mark of grace and the call to discipleship stamped on every day of our lives.

DEATH'S DESTRUCTION
ISAIAH 25:6-9

"On this mountain, the LORD of hosts will make for all peoples / a feast of rich food, a feast of well-aged wines" (Isaiah 25:6). The church has traditionally heard these words of Isaiah through the lens of our high feast of Easter. The feast that Isaiah saw from afar was a party, an extravagant banquet of celebration. We Protestants may have too much of the Puritan in us to appreciate the excesses of God's table. In Hebrew, *rich food* means "fat" or "oil." Likewise, the wine cellars will be raided for this feast, not for the discounted gallon jugs but for the choice flasks still dusty because no one could afford them. God's extravagance at the feast on this mountain derives from the extravagance of God's actions that are celebrated.

Isaiah said that God would "destroy on this mountain / the shroud that is cast over all peoples, / the sheet that is spread over all nations" (verse 7). Little wonder the church turned to this text for Easter's celebration. Jesus' resurrection destroys death. Isaiah did not live to see the resurrection of Jesus, but he did live to trust and risk its anticipation.

I say "risk" because one might well imagine that the initial reaction to Isaiah's words about death's destruction paralleled the first responses to Noah's hammering together of timbers. Laughter. Ridicule. How can you say such a thing when death is the one constant in life?

Death and its fear shroud the whole of our lives. We feel death's chill in the passing of loved ones. We see death's threat in those who wield death to enforce conformity to their will. We fear death's power to overtake us, to strip us of the relationships we most cherish and the experiences we find most exhilarating. These are chills, threats, and fears that belong to our day as surely as they did to Isaiah's times. If death is not undone, all the other crises we face pale in comparison. All the other joys we share prove short-lived.

Yet, according to Isaiah's promise, God "will swallow up death forever" (verse 8). That is a curious turn of words. God's destruction of death does not come at arm's length by God unleashing overwhelming power from a safe distance. God will "swallow up death forever." The destruction comes at close range by swallowing, by ingesting, by God taking death's power into God's own self. In the cross of Christ, God suffers from the inside what pains us in death. On a hillside (or to keep to Isaiah's imagery, a mountain) outside Jerusalem, the first act of God swallowing up death occurred when Christ entered death's jaws. The death was real, as was its grief.

Mary's grief in the garden is poignant. "They have taken away my Lord, and I do not know where they have laid him" (John 20:13). The disciples' grief was mixed with fear and guilt. On Easter evening, even after hearing Mary's stunning report, John reported that "the doors of the house where the disciples had met were locked for fear" (John 20:19). Mary grieved. The disciples grieved. But God? Have you ever wondered about the grief of God in that time between the Crucifixion and the Resurrection? Can you imagine God's tears?

"Then the Lord GOD will wipe away the tears from all faces" (Isaiah 25:8). Perhaps God understands the importance of wiping away grief's tears because of God's own grief for the suffering and death of Jesus. "It will be said on that day, / Lo, this is our God; we have waited for him, so that he might save us" (verse 9). *Waiting* and *salvation*: Isaiah paired these two words together over 2,700 years ago. Waiting and salvation remain paired in our time. We celebrate the feast of Easter as a banquet of

grace that revels in death's undoing, but that undoing is not yet complete. Faith remains trust. We are not yet at the top of this mountain foreseen by Isaiah. We still climb to reach its heights. As we do, most of the time all we can see is the slope ahead of us. The switchbacks stretch beyond our eyesight. We may wonder, *Will we ever reach the top? Will we ever see what Isaiah sees: God's feast, death's destruction, and the end of tears?*

Waiting and salvation remain the hallmarks of our faith, but ours is not a waiting that consists of inaction. Ours is a waiting that involves faithful and trusting action. We wait for God's salvation as those who seek to transform this age in which we live by the qualities and characteristics of God's awaited realm. We wait for God's salvation as servants of God.

From the vantage point of Easter, on the top of Isaiah's mountain, we see the promised feast of rich foods and well-aged wines. Looking back and around in this world awaiting salvation, however, we cannot avoid the sight of brothers and sisters around us who starve for food and thirst for hope. Easter's celebration spurs us to share from the abundance with which God blesses this world and our lives. Our calling as servants of the risen Lord is to offer as the Spirit makes possible the bounties of God's feast to those who go without.

Likewise, from the vantage point of Easter, on the top of Isaiah's mountain, we see death's promised destruction. However, looking back and around in this world awaiting salvation, we cannot avoid seeing how death still exercises its dominion. We see that dominion in our own mortality and that of our loved ones. We see that dominion struggling to maintain a foothold among those who use death as a bludgeon against others, who give no thought to innocent victims or rationalize their demise under the euphemism of "collateral damage." Such deathly specters cast a killing shroud over a day intended for joy and life. Then again, that is precisely the sort of backdrop from which the first Easter broke free. Just as the first disciples struggled to move out from under the weight of crucifixion into resurrection faith, so our Easter faith must find a way for its message to confront those who trade in death.

The Christ we serve suffered crucifixion, unjustly and innocently; and he calls us to look for the innocents who suffer in our day. Any one who would serve Christ is called to respond to serve and shelter those innocents. Any one who would speak for the risen Christ will speak on behalf of those innocents. The words of the king in Jesus' parable echo, "Truly I tell you, just as you did it to one of the least of these who are members of my family, you did it to me" (Matthew 25:40).

"This is the LORD for whom we have waited; / let us be glad and rejoice in his salvation" (Isaiah 25:9). Easter serves as the preliminary sounding of that refrain, as much in praise of God as in defiance of death. To the innocents who suffer, those who languish in the grip of Alzheimers or AIDS, all of us who grieve the death of loved ones and edge uneasily toward our own passing, Easter shouts that these things are not the final word. The final word, as it is in Isaiah's passage, is God's salvation. In Hebrew, the word for "salvation" is *yeshuah*, the root word for the name *Jesus*. The final word for us is not the somber solemnity of Good Friday's vigil. The final word for us is a feast, a face wiped clean of tears, a crucified and risen Jesus who has swallowed up death forever. As we hope, so may we live.

What does it mean to you to know that God has swallowed up death? In what ways does the resurrection of Jesus influence your life of faith?

THE GOSPEL'S CORE
1 CORINTHIANS 15:1-11

The entire first letter to the Corinthians has been marked with Paul addressing various disputes in the community. Some we know all too well from our own experiences: cliques that form around personalities (Chapter 3). Some conflicts seem far removed from our experience: issues of whether or not food sacrificed to idols should be eaten (Chapters 8–11). Then there are disputes over matters of marriage and sexuality (Chapter 7) and inappropriate conduct at the Lord's Supper (11:17-34).

In Chapter 15, Paul reminds the church of Corinth of the core teaching of their faith: the Resurrection. The opening verse asserts this core by way of repetition in language. "Good news" translates the Greek *euaggelion*, a noun also translated as "gospel" elsewhere. "Proclaimed" translates the Greek *euaggelizo*. So if we had a corresponding verb in English, Paul began by calling attention to the "gospel" that I "gospeled" to you. The use of that same verb again in verse 2 simply adds to the direction of Paul's argument: This is the gospel we are talking about.

What is the core of this gospel—or as Paul put it in verse 3, what is "of first importance?" (1) Christ died for our sins in accordance with the Scriptures; (2) Christ was buried; and (3) Christ was raised on the third day in accordance with the Scriptures. It is important to keep in mind that this threefold core of the gospel revealed in the Resurrection is not something that is original to Paul. He asserted that this core that he "handed on" to the Corinthians had itself been received by him. "Handed on" in verse 3 is the same verb Paul used in 11:23 to speak of the tradition he handed on regarding the Lord's Supper, a tradition that Paul, again, said that he received. As a result, many hear in this summation of the gospel, as in the traditions of the Lord's Supper, an early Christian confession that made its way through those originating communities.

Beyond an affirmation of this early Christian confession, these words remind us of the nature of Christian faith and proclamation in every era. We stand in the midst of a long series of those who have received faith's gift and then passed it on. The celebration of Easter reminds us that the gift and promise of new life seeks such handing on by us. Easter is not our private celebration. Easter is God's gift and promise to the world. Those who claim and are claimed by Easter's faith and grace find ourselves called to throw the doors and windows wide open so others might hear the glad news and join in the joy of this day and its promise for all days to come.

Having stated the core principles of the gospel grounded in resurrection faith, Paul moved to a listing of witnesses, those to whom Christ had appeared. Paul framed the list in a way that combines the authority of persons with the sheer weight of numbers. Cephas (the Aramaic name for *Peter*) heads the list, and why not? By this time Peter was generally believed to be the leading authority figure in the church, at least outside of Jerusalem where James still was highly regarded (and James is included in this list of witnesses). Next, the Twelve are noted (Peter being one of them). Then Paul made reference to more than five hundred. Finally, at the end, Paul added himself as one of those to whom Christ had appeared.

While the Easter epistle reading ends here, Paul's teachings on resurrection continue through the end of Chapter 15. He argued against those who question whether resurrection is central to faith. Paul offered words that sought to shed light on what sort of life resurrection might involve. Finally, Paul asserted in a way similar to the earlier passage from Isaiah that the resurrection of Jesus had won a decisive victory over death.

For now, however, in this passage, Paul laid the groundwork for all that would follow. The whole of the gospel turns on the death and resurrection of Jesus by God for our sake. Our practice of that gospel in love of God and for one another has its basis and its hope in that core proclamation of God's power to raise life out of death. The appearances of the risen Jesus afford the hope that we, like the Corinthians of old, may believe not in vain but in trust: trust in the God who raised Jesus, trust that we like Christ are held in God's gracious and saving hands. Christ is risen!

How does Paul's understanding of the gospel compare to your own? What will the prayers, the music, the liturgy, and other elements of your church's service on Easter Sunday reveal to you as the core of resurrection faith?

"I HAVE SEEN"
JOHN 20:1-20

Easter begins among the tombs and in the dark. Those are not merely the literary settings of place and time with which John and the other Gospel writers began their Easter narratives. Easter begins, if it is to begin at all, in our times and places where death still claims the last word and light still seems all but obliterated from view.

Where are those places today? Consider the question from your own experience. As you look out upon the world around you and as you look in upon the world inside of you, where do struggle to see for lack of light? Where do you run into brick walls erected by the dyings of hope or justice or compassion? Where do you find your-self grieving for what has been but is no more? If you want to discern where Easter begins, those are the places you and I must go. How can we find hope and joy in a cemetery or when all is darkness? Easter celebrates our ability to see into and beyond the darkness into the light of the risen Christ.

The story in John's Gospel begins with the discovery of a stone rolled away from a tomb. On that first Easter morning, Mary Magdalene went to the tomb of a loved one now dead. She went with every footstep made heavy with grief. She went in the dark. Mary took that risk, and she saw. Granted, at the beginning, she did not see much. She saw that the stone was removed from the tomb. Mary did not see resurrection, but Mary did see that something had changed; and she did not welcome the change. Yet she took another risk. She ran back to tell the others. Curiously, she did not tell them what she had seen, a stone rolled away. Instead, Mary told them, "They have taken the Lord out of the tomb, and we do not know where they have laid him" (John 20:2). Mary had seen the stone rolled away, but that is not what she reported. Mary told them what she feared had happened.

There are times it is like that for us. We tell others not so much what we see as what we think or fear it means. We imagine the worst that can happen. We do not have a sense of the whole but only part of it.

Mary's report, however, became the catalyst for urgent action. The Easter narrative steps away from Mary momentarily to speak of two disciples who heard her report:

Simon Peter and "the other disciple." They ran together to see the tomb, and the other disciple outran Peter and arrived first. He looked inside and saw the linen cloths but not the body. Peter went inside the tomb; and he, too, saw the linen cloths. They, like Mary, saw. In fact, they saw quite a bit more than she saw. John's Gospel tells us, "Then the other disciple, who reached the tomb first, also went in, and he saw and believed" (verse 8). However, in an extraordinary twist, after seeing and even after the other disciple believed, they said nothing. "For as yet they did not understand the scripture, that he must rise from the dead" (verse 9). They went home.

The church can respond in ways that are similar to the actions of Peter and the other disciple. Our churches on Easter may be soaked with the aromas of blooming white lilies that decorate chancels with their trumpet-like blossoms. The choirs proclaim the resurrection of Christ with choruses of alleluias. We stand and joyfully sing the hymn "Christ the Lord Is Risen Today." However, are we as good at getting Easter out of *our* sanctuary homes as we are at celebrating Easter inside the sanctuary?

Do we run together out of sanctuaries in search of someone, *anyone*, who would listen to our proclamation: Do you know what? Christ is risen! Do we pour out of those doors filled with Resurrection energy to bring life to people caught in those deadly and depressing places we considered earlier at the beginning of this study? Or, like those two disciples, do we return to our homes, having seen much, but

having said little if anything outside the safety of sanctuaries? Maybe that is why John abruptly halted the narrative of these two. It is unclear what they did and why. Did John wait on us to answer the question for them and for ourselves?

In the garden, with Mary back in the scene, several remarkable things happened. To begin with, John stopped using the word *tomb*. Why? John shifted from a setting focused on death to one of life. Mary's eyes and sight initially failed her as she mistook Jesus for a gardener. She continued to believe that someone had taken Jesus' body, and perhaps it was this gardener. "Sir, if you have carried him away, tell me where you have laid him, and I will take him away" (verse 15). However, when she heard her name spoken as no other spoke it, Mary recognized Jesus. She became the first witness of the resurrected Jesus. "I have seen the Lord" (verse 18).

Easter bloomed for Mary when the risen Jesus spoke her name. Jesus instructed her to tell the others, "I am ascending to my Father and your Father, to my God and your God." That may be the way we all finally come to Easter faith. It is not by persuasive argument about the logical possibility of such an event. It is certainly not by scientific explanations of how resurrection happens, on which the Gospels are silent. Easter comes by hearing our name spoken by the risen One. Easter brings into being the truth of relationship with the Risen One. It offers the hope that all our relationships can be transformed by the power that transforms death and calls forth life. Once we recognize that Easter is our story as well as the church's story, then, like Mary, we see. Seeing, we become living testaments. We are called to tell our brothers and sisters the good news of the risen Christ.

"I have seen the Lord." With those words the Magdalene became the first of the disciples sent by Jesus to announce God's raising of Christ for the sake of the world. Thanks be to God for this Easter day and for its transforming of all our days!

Where in your life is Easter's light and hope most needed at this moment? In what ways might you celebrate Easter in mission as well as in liturgy, in service as well as in song?